To Beth –

Candy wonderful to

Share this memory ...

... Love

Regard Mort 2015

Regina's Table

At

Twin Oaks

Regina
Trosclair
Charboneau

CONTENTS

Foreword

"Feeding is loving" at least that's the mantra in the South, where I grew up. Reared on tomato sandwiches, cheese grits, and fried chicken, I was taught the value of sharing expression through food at a young age— banana bread for the new neighbors, chicken pot pie for the new parents, sour cream pound cake for anyone who'd lost a loved one, and vegetables from the garden for anyone who didn't have their own. For the Southerner, it is a sixth sense; one known around the world, as we Southerners have always known, the sense of *hospitality.*

No one knows the art of hospitality better than Regina Charboneau, chef extraordinaire, bon vivant, gracious hostess, and loyal friend to those of us blessed to know her and call her a friend. I first met Regina in San Francisco, far from my home birthplace in Mississippi. I had lived in the city for just over a year, not long enough to lose my Southern accent– but long enough to grow a little homesick for my roots. I was traveling up and down the West Coast, writing about the food and lifestyle of its people, yet I was missing the food and lifestyle of the South. I needed a taste of home. A friend recommended Biscuits & Blues, a restaurant just off Union Square, started by a darling woman from Mississippi who, my friend added, "makes a mean bowl of gumbo." I got more than a perfect roux that night, because it was then and there that I got my first serving of Regina.

It was as if we'd known one another for years. She greeted me at my table, discovered our common birthplace, and asked if she could join me. It didn't matter that Van Morrison was a few tables away wanting to compliment her on the menu. Regina was all mine that night. We made it from biscuits to bread pudding without taking a breath. The two of us sat for hours, telling stories about life and love and home sweet home. Such is the case with Southerners–we gather around food and let go and lose our inhibitions. We spill our stories and divulge our dreams over breakfast, lunch, and dinner.

Regina's story was a good one. She had spent her fair share of time in the City by the Bay starting one of San Francisco's most beloved restaurants, Regina's at the Regis Hotel. She had lived everywhere from Alaska to Paris by the time she landed in California. But there was only one place in the world she wanted to raise her boys, Luc and Martin, that was back home in Natchez, Mississippi.

And so she and her husband, Doug, bought Twin Oaks, a marvelous antebellum home in Natchez, which they have lovingly restored. Regina started cooking class weekends where guests could stay in her charming guest rooms that are located in an original dependency on the property and have a class with Regina, which included consuming the end product in her lovely dining room. The guest rooms had a second purpose ~ her friends, who mean the world to her, would come from all over the world to rest and be wrapped in food and love like nowhere else but in Regina's care.

One Christmas, the holidays drew me home to Mississippi. Regina had insisted I come down for a night during my visit home for the holidays. "Bring your mother and your appetite," she insisted, "we'll have a girls' weekend." Regina and her mother greeted us with open arms–and an open bottle of fantastic Cabernet. The four of us sat in her parlor for hours; I remember I felt a keen sense of place that night. I didn't know whether it was Twin Oaks or Regina, or some mixture medley of the two, but this was the South I loved and cherished. This was the South I missed. Continued....

I came back time and time again and, on one of these visits, Regina and I walked out to the front of Twin Oaks where two enormous oak trees reigned-the property's namesakes. Some 300 years old, the trees grew side by side until their branches intertwined. I thought it was just about the most romantic picture in the world. "When you meet the right man, you'll come back here to Twin Oaks, and you'll get married under these trees," she said.

It took more time to meet the right man than it did for me to agree to her idea. Regina gave her thumbs up when she met Greg one night, back in San Francisco, at Biscuits & Blues. "He's the one," she said. "Don't let him get away." I held on tight and, when we were engaged, I put forward my little plan. We would marry at Regina's, under the two oak trees, and we'd introduce all of our friends to the South that was my home. There was only one woman who could pull off a perfect Southern welcome for so many urbanites, and it was Regina. I could depend on Regina to shower our friends from London, New York, and San Francisco with the kind of hospitality they'd never forget.

Regina's known for pouring out graciousness. She has fed famous faces-Lily Tomlin, Shirley MacLaine, Tim Curry and Anderson Cooper are among many. And she's fed with the same care and love the not-so-famous such as the locals in the daily Coffee group, a Thursday night poker club or those Louisianans displaced by Hurricane Katrina in nearby New Orleans who have become her dearest of friends. She's spent languid evenings throughout the summer feeding hot dogs and homemade chili to all the neighborhood kids every Wednesday when her boys were younger. Then there was time for Regina's friends with Wednesday's Wine group. She's entertained the varied guests of birthday girls and brides (I'm happy to count myself one of them). No matter who sits at her table, Regina makes them feel like family.

And she creates every menu as if it were a little novella, the ingredients like small chapters in a lovely little story. I remember every meal I've ever eaten with Regina, just as I remember the best lines in books I've cherished. I'm confident when the pages of this cookbook are well worn, smudged with Regina's unique style of southern cooking, you too will come to count this cookbook as so much more than a compendium of Regina's recipes. To understand this cookbook-and taste these recipes-is to be loved by the sweetest woman I know-and be a part of the sweetest home of all. Here's to never-ending helpings of grace, hospitality, generosity, and Southern love.
Thank you Regina.

Paige Porter Fischer
San Francisco, California
2007

Twin Oaks

Twin Oaks has hosted so many dinners through the years it is hard to imagine how many meals were cooked, how many times tables were set and how many guests were served in nearly two hundred years. I often look at old photos and try to imagine what may have been served during the time the Evans, Morris, Connelly, Davis, Dubuisson, Dunbar , Gastrell, Barton and Whittington families called Twin Oaks home.

The Whittingtons lived here the longest, from 1940-1999. One of the daughters of Dr. Homer and Elizabeth Whittington has shared many stories of times here at Twin Oaks, from the French Ambassador's Dinner where her father feared the Tomato Aspic would melt because the guests were running late, to her Grand Ball in 1954 when she was Queen of Pilgrimage and the weather turned cold and the guests danced every where in the house, including in the bath tub. Her parents were known for their hospitality and Crepes Suzette. I have included a recipe for Crepes Suzette in my New Year's menu in memory of Dr. Whittington. When Rena Jean remembers her mother, Elizabeth, she laughs recalling how her mother planned her menu in between the guests names. A course for her menu would come up between the names of couples. She also shared that Dr. Whittington referred to the room we call "The Bar" as "The Recovery Room". That name came from hosting many tourists during the time Twin Oaks was on tour during Pilgrimage. At the end of a long tour day they would gather in "The Recovery Room" for mint juleps and such. I love her stories and it just reminds me why we love opening our home to friends and family. It is just the kind of home that Twin Oaks is and I imagine it always has been.

INTRODUCTION

At your first glance at this book you will see complete menus for entertaining during each of the four seasons, with recipes. This book consists of five elements, but only four that you will visibly see; The Art of Seasonal Cooking; Complete Menus; Recipes with a Southern accent running through most of them and the history and feel of my home, Twin Oaks.

The fifth element may only exist for me; every recipe and every menu of this book conjures up memories of parties I have had and people I love. I chose not to write about guest lists and details that might become tedious to someone who was not there at the time. Many of my family and friends will recognize a menu or menu item immediately and, hopefully, will have a good memory attached. I will admit I have had an advantage, simply from being born and raised in Natchez, Mississippi. Southern hospitality is second nature to me. I am not the exception but more of the rule-being one of many fine hosts and hostesses in this charming River Town. As it often happens in a small town, I spent the first twenty three years of my life trying to get away from Natchez and spent the next twenty three trying to get back. Once I returned and experienced my sons growing up here, I now understand why my mother's family has been here for seven generations. My boys are now a part of the eighth generation and I hope they will come to understand how special that is. It took me many years to realize how special being born in Natchez truly is. My parents were both profound teachers of loving people and life. My mother is a gracious hostess and always has been, but truly good food came into our family through marriage. My father, J.P. Trosclair, was the quintessential South Louisianan; never an empty pot and never an empty home. The Sunday lunches at our house always provided the best food of the season which in turn brought the best company and conversation to our table. I am simply carrying on the tradition. When I found my way to Paris, LaVarenne was there for the fundamentals which are essential. But truly, the Paris experience that shaped me was sitting at the table of Arlette Romand. Arlette lends a unique style to all that she touches: food, table, family and friends. I credit Arlette for adding a little French to the Southern style my mother, Frances, so graciously gave me. There are so many people in my life that have added to my knowledge and sense of style especially our family friend, Loveta Byrne, a fabulous cook and Tim Curry a fabulous friend and one of the most comfortable hosts I know.

After having interesting but brief stints at three or four Southern Colleges in the early nineteen seventies, I found myself headed to Alaska with a group of friends from Louisiana State University. *That is a book in itself, left in the bathroom of a Chevron Station in Missoula, Montana by an angry ex; a plane crash in the bush of Alaska; a marriage proposal consisting of "you can paint the house any color you want and I won't beat you...very much" (I declined), and cooking at construction camps in the bush of Alaska to save money to go to school in France. I apologize to my Mother for any early aging.*

After returning to Alaska from Paris and becoming the first woman chef for Club Corporation of America at the Tower Club in Anchorage I went on to open restaurants. Each restaurant had a time and a reason–Alaska, San Francisco, Sonoma even a Blues Club in San Francisco-Biscuits and Blues. My favorite will always be Regina's in the Regis Hotel in the Theater District on Geary Street in San Francisco. It was then that I realized how deep my southern roots were and it was reflected in my cuisine. My southern roots help define my style and my Cuisine most definitely had a Southern accent with a French twist.

Although there are a few favorite recipes from my restaurants and home in San Francisco as well as some of my dinner parties in New York, over all, the book is reflective of my Natchez life where I always know who I am. "Twin Oaks" has made coming back all make sense-it is a home to be shared. As always, I entertain quite often. It does not matter whether I am hosting the Opera gala, grilling hot dogs for my boys and their friends, or my table is laden with fresh flowers and I am serving a formal dinner; Twin Oaks is filled with the aroma of good food, conversation and laughter and for me an overwhelming feeling of love, happiness and contentment of being at home. No doubt, I did bring a little Paris, San Francisco and New York back home to Natchez, but the fact is I always brought a whole lot of Natchez to wherever I went. I hope through this book you will find enough to help you develop your own style to enjoy cooking and entertaining as much as I do.

Welcome to my Table at Twin Oaks—

Regina

Spring Menus

Summer Menus

Fall Menus

Winter Menus

Spring at Twin Oaks

Keep in mind there is always a reason and always a season to visit Natchez.

Two of the most popular Seasons to visit Natchez are during the Spring and Fall. In Spring the flowers are abundant. The Natchez Spring Pilgrimage is a tour of Antebellum Houses and has been hosted by the local Garden Clubs for over 76 years. In May each year we have the Natchez Festival of Music with Jazz, Broadway Musicals and a major focus on Opera. Twin Oaks has often hosted the closing night gala and it has lasted until the wee hours so the Artists that visit from all over have their chance for good byes.

When my friends visit in Spring to tour the houses of Natchez, of course, I entertain them "Natchez Style". In Natchez we love brunches and we especially like a brunch with Milk Punch. When I entertain I like to join in the party so when I plan a menu I keep that in mind. For this menu the Beignet Dough can be made ahead and even rolled out, the Ham & Endive Salad can be prepared the day before. I will share my technique for pre-making omelets and finishing them in the oven so you are not tied to the stove. The bread pudding mix can be made ahead but I prefer baking it off so they are hot when you serve them.

I always set my table and arrange my flowers a day ahead. I can hardly start cooking until the mood for my party is set. It seems to inspire me to be more focused in the kitchen, knowing when guests walk in I will look ready...even if I am not completely done in the kitchen. Your guests can always have a Brandy Milk Punch while you are putting your finishing touches on your menu.

Natchez Style

Brandy Milk Punch

- 3 oz. Brandy
  (the better the Brandy the better the drink)
- 1 cup whole Milk
- 3 teaspoon Powdered Sugar
- 2 cups of Ice Cubes

This recipe makes 4 Drinks

Use a blender- add two cups of Ice, add Brandy and blend for 15-20 seconds. Add Milk and Powdered Sugar and blend for another 15 seconds. Strain into stemmed glass.
Nutmeg is traditional but optional. White Crème de Cacao is not traditional but I often add two tablespoons for more sweetness and flavor for a variation. My preference is au natural with just the Brandy, Milk and Sugar.

Spring Brunch
Menu

Brandy Milk Punch

Beignets
dusted in Powdered Sugar

Endive, Apple & Ham Salad
with Lemon Mustard Vinaigrette

White Cheddar Omelets
with Crab & Onion Topping

Bananas Foster Bread Pudding
with Vanilla Ice Cream

ENDIVE, APPLE & HAM SALAD

Ingredients for Endive, Apple and Ham Salad

- 1 lb.   Endive (Belgium white or Italian red tipped)
- 2 cups   Diced Tart Apples
- 2 cups   Diced Ham
- 1/2 cup   Diced Red Onion
- 2   Boiled Eggs for garnish
- 1/3 cup   Lemon Mustard Vinaigrette

MAKES 8 SERVINGS

There is often confusion between Endive and Chicory. They are from the same family. What you want for this Salad is the pale, compact, spear shaped one that the French and Belgians call Endive. It is available in most grocery stores but for certain in the specialty produce stores such as Whole Foods. Chicory, also known as Frisee, is a dense, curly green. If Endive is not available it can be used as a suitable substitute for the recipe.

1- Before chopping all the Endive, reserve a few leaves for garnish.

2- Cut Endive in half length-wise, then in 1/2 inch slices. Toss with diced Apples, Red Onion and Ham.

3- Toss in Salad Dressing and garnish with whole Endive leaves and sliced Boiled Eggs.

LEMON MUSTARD VINAIGRETTE

MAKES 8 SERVINGS

1- In food processor or blender put in Dijon Mustard and Vinegar, then mix for a few seconds.

2- Take a fresh Lemon and squeeze two tablespoons of Juice. Add to blender.

3- Add Salt, Sugar and Shallot. Puree for a few seconds.

4- Turn on food processor and slowly add Salad Oil. (Vinaigrette should be creamy).

5- Add a little of this Dressing at a time to Salad. Toss and coat ingredients well. You want to coat all of the ingredients, but you don't want excess Dressing.

Ingredients for Lemon Mustard Vinaigrette

- 2 tbls.   Dijon Mustard
- 2 tbls.   White Vinegar
- 2 tbls.   Fresh Lemon Juice
- 1/2 teas.   Salt
- 1 tbls.   Sugar
- 1   Shallot
- 1/2 cup   Salad Oil

New Orleans Style Beignets

MAKES 2 DOZEN BEIGNETS

1- In mixing bowl put in Flour, packet of Dry Yeast and Sugar.

2- In small sauce pan heat Milk, Water and Butter until Butter has almost melted. Cool down to 120 degrees before adding to the Flour mixture in the mixing bowl. The warm Milk mixture should be no more than 120 degrees. Mix with dough hook on medium speed for two minutes.

3- Add Egg Yolk and Vanilla to the Dough mixture and mix for another minute.

4- The Dough should be soft but not sticking to the sides. *If Dough is too soft you may need to add a little more Flour to get the consistency you need. If the Dough seems too stiff add a teaspoon of warm Water at a time until Dough is soft but not sticking.*

5- In large metal bowl add 1 teas. of Salad Oil. Turn Dough out into this bowl. Flip Dough over to coat both sides. Cover with a dry towel or plastic wrap (not air tight, loose).

6- Let Dough rise for one hour at room temperature or overnight in the refrigerator.

7- On Floured surface, roll Dough out to 1/4 inch thick. Cut into 2 1/2 inch x 3 inch rectangles.

8- Heat Oil to 350 degrees. Put Beignets in a few at a time. When they begin to puff up gently turn over and brown other side. Both sides should be a light golden brown.

9- Drain on paper towel. Dust with Powdered Sugar. Serve as soon as possible. They are best served hot.

If you are having a crowd you can fry off Beignets earlier. Do not dust with Sugar. Reheat in 350 degree oven for 5 minutes, dust with Sugar and serve

Ingredients for Beignets	
2 1/2 cups	Flour
1/2 cup	Flour (to roll out Beignets)
1 pkg.	Active Dry Yeast
3 tbls.	Sugar
3 tbls.	Butter
1/4 cup	Milk
1/4 cup	Warm Water
1	Egg Yolk
1 teas.	Vanilla
1 cup	Powdered Sugar
1 qt.	Oil for Frying

WHITE CHEDDAR OMELETS

MAKES 8 SERVINGS

You need a good 6 inch non-stick egg pan. You will also need a rubber spatula. I use 3 eggs per Omelet for an Entrée.

1- In mixing bowl put in 24 Eggs, add the Cream, Salt and minced Garlic.

2- Blend with a fork until the Eggs are creamy yellow, about 1 minute.

3- Warm non-stick egg pan, put over medium heat. You don't want your pan too hot. A perfect Omelet is not browned at all. It should be golden yellow.

4- Place 1 tablespoon of Butter into Egg pan.

5- Pour 2 oz. (or 1/4 cup) of Egg mixture into pan. Lift pan and swirl mixture around pan. Let sit on heat for 30 seconds. Take rubber spatula and lift Omelet to let uncooked Egg mixture flow to bottom.

6- Put in 1 oz. of grated White Cheddar and fold Omelet over.

7- Remove from pan and place on serving platter. Repeat for the next 7 Omelets. Keep covered with clean kitchen towel to keep warm until serving.

When I am entertaining a crowd, I make my Omelets ahead of time. I cook them half way and lift round Omelet onto a greased cookie sheet, add my cheese and finish in 350 degree oven right before serving. Make sure your Crab Topping is good and hot.

Ingredients for White Cheddar Omelets		
•	24	Eggs
•	1/4 cup	Cream
•	1/4 teas.	Salt
•	1/8 teas.	Minced Garlic
•	8 tbls.	Butter
•	16 oz.	Grated White Cheddar

CRAB & ONION TOPPING

MAKES 8 SERVINGS

1- In large sauté pan melt Butter over medium heat. Let Butter melt, but not brown.

2- Add julienne of Onion and continue to cook over medium heat. Cook until they are limp and transparent, but not brown.

3- Add Green Onions, Basil and fresh Lemon Juice.

4- Add Crab Meat and cook for 1 minute.

5- Spoon Crab topping evenly over the top of the Omelets on the serving dish.

If you like a spicy dish, you may add 1/4 teaspoon of Crushed Red Pepper Flakes.

Ingredients for Crab and Onion Topping		
•	1 lb.	Lump Crab Meat
•	1/4 lb.	Butter
•	1/2 cup	Minced Green Onion
•	1/2 cup	Julienne Onion
•	3 tbls.	Minced Fresh Basil
•	2 tbls.	Fresh Lemon Juice

BASIC BREAD PUDDING

MAKES 8 SERVINGS
You will need a 9x11 baking pan or 8 individual custard cups. Spray with Oil or coat with melted Butter or Margarine.

1- Place Eggs, Cream and Brown Sugar in a large mixing bowl. Using a hand mixer, beat Eggs, Brown Sugar and Cream together on medium speed for two minutes.

2- Add Cinnamon, Grated Orange.

3- Fold in Cubed Bread and Pecans. Using a spoon or spatula make sure all Bread is coated with the Batter.

4- Pour into Buttered baking dish. Bake at 350 degrees for 45-50 minutes.

5- Let cool down for ten minutes before cutting into eight squares. Place on individual dessert plates.

6- Top each square with Vanilla Ice Cream and Bananas Foster Topping.

Ingredients for Basic Bread Pudding

•	2 cups	Cream
•	6	Eggs
•	1 cup	Brown Sugar
•	1 teas.	Cinnamon
•	1 teas.	Grated Orange
•	4 cups	Cubed Bread
•	1/2 cup	Pecans

Ingredients for Bananas Foster Topping

•	4	Bananas
•	1/4 lb.	Butter
•	1 cup	Brown Sugar
•	1 teas.	Fresh Lemon Juice
•	1 tbls.	Fresh Orange Juice
•	1 teas.	Orange Zest
•	2 tbls.	Dark Rum
•	1/4 teas.	Cinnamon
•	1 qt.	Vanilla Ice Cream

BANANAS FOSTER TOPPING

MAKES 8 SERVINGS

1- In large sauté pan, over medium heat, melt Butter, then add Brown Sugar.

2- Add Lemon Juice, Orange Juice and Orange Zest (if you don't have a zester you can finely grate the Orange Peel). Continue to cook until Brown Sugar has cooked to a Syrup.

3- Peel Bananas, cut Banana length-wise, then in thirds. You want the pieces to be about two inches each. Add Bananas to Brown Sugar Syrup in the pan.

4- Add the Rum and Cinnamon. Heat for just about 45 seconds. You want the Bananas to remain firm.

5- Spoon warm Bananas in Rum flavored Syrup over Vanilla Ice Cream.

Spring Cooking Class at Twin Oaks

Menu

Salad of
Watercress, Mache & Foie Gras
in Mustard Vinaigrette

Poulet Grand-Mere
Roasted Baby Carrots, Turnips
and Potatoes with Lemon Balm

Baked Onions in Cream

Chocolate Mousse Torte
with Orange Scented Crème Anglaise

Salad of Watercress, Mache & Foie Gras

MAKES 6 SERVINGS

1- In blender add Shallot, Vinegar, Mustard, Salt and Sugar. Blend for a few seconds. Add Oil slowly to emulsify (or thicken).

2- Wash and dry Watercress and Mache.

3- Pour a little Dressing at a time and toss to coat the Salad leaves.

4- Arrange tossed Salad onto 6 chilled salad plates.

5- Slice the Foie Gras into 6 pieces. Place one piece on top of each Salad.

6- Garnish with Sliced Egg and toasted French Bread rounds.

There are several imported brands of Foie Gras or Foie du Canard (which is from Duck). The Duck is often 30% less expensive. It is very good as well. If you want to use a mousse style domestic pate it is a wonderful substitute for this Salad without the expense.

Ingredients for Mustard Vinaigrette	
• 1	Shallot
• 1/4 cup	Cider Vinegar
• 1 tbls.	Dijon Mustard
• 1/2 cup	Salad Oil
• 1/2 teas.	Salt
• 1 teas.	Sugar

Ingredients For Salad with Foie Gras

- 1 bunch   Watercress
- 1 lb.   Mache (*also known as Lambs Lettuce*). *If not available substitute more Watercress and some mixed Baby Lettuce.*
- 6 oz.   Bloc Foie Gras Terrine
- 12   Toasted slices of Baguette
- 3   Boiled Eggs

Ingredients for Baked Onions in Cream	
• 6	Medium Onions
• 1/4 lb.	Butter
• 1/2 pint	Cream
• 1/4 teas.	Nutmeg

The picture on top of the Menu is a penny postcard that a friend found in an antique post-card shop. I love having printed menus for my Dinner parties. I often scan a piece of Art from my house and use it in my menus.

Baked Onions in Cream

MAKES 6 SERVINGS

1- Cut off tops of Onion and peel to the first white layer of the Onion.

2- Arrange in porcelain baking dish.

3- Put 1 tbls. of Butter on top of each Onion.

4- Add Cream and Nutmeg.

5- Cover with foil and bake at 350 degrees for 80 to 90 minutes. The Onions should be tender but not falling apart.

Poulet Grand-Mere (grandmother's chicken)

MAKES 6 SERVINGS

Use roasting pan that has a lid.
Preheat oven to 425 Degrees.

1- Rinse and dry Fryers, place in Roasting Pan that has a cover.

2- Cover Chicken with bottle of White Wine and 1 cup of Water.

3- Add Horseradish, Garlic, Salt and White Pepper.

4- Cook for 30 minutes uncovered then turn Oven down to 350 degrees and cover and cook for another 60 minutes.

5- Pour liquid from Roasting Pan into a 3 qt. Sauce Pan.

6- Reduce over medium to high heat until you have 2 cups of liquid.

7- Add 1 pint of Heavy Cream and reduce until you have approx. 2 cups of liquid.

8- Slowly whisk in soft Butter using about a tablespoon at a time.

9- Remove skin from Chicken and remove Breasts from bones, slice and place on serving platter.

10- Remove Thighs and take out thigh bone and arrange meat on serving platter with Breast meat.

11- Remove Wings and place on platter.

12- Pour Sauce over Chicken on platter and put extra sauce in gravy boat to place on table.

13- Garnish with Roasted Vegetables.

Ingredients for Grandmother's Chicken		
•	2 each	3 lb. Fryers
•	1 bottle	White Wine
•	1 cup	Water
•	1/2 cup	Prepared Horseradish
•	2 tbls.	Minced Garlic
•	3 tbls.	Salt
•	1 tbls.	White Pepper
	For finishing Sauce	
•	1 pint	Heavy Cream
•	1/4 lb.	Butter

Ingredients for Roasted Vegetables		
•	2 tbls.	Olive Oil
•	8	Garlic Cloves
•	18	Baby Carrots
•	12	Baby Turnips
•	18	Baby New Red Potatoes
•	6 leaves	Fresh Lemon Balm
•		Salt and Pepper to taste

Roasted Baby Carrots, Turnips & Potatoes

MAKES 6 SERVINGS
Preheat oven to 425 degrees.

1- In heavy roaster toss the Garlic, Peeled Baby Carrots, Peeled Baby Turnips and skin on Potatoes with Olive Oil, Salt and Pepper.

2- Roast in 425 degree oven for 25 minutes. Use a spatula to turn the Vegetables so they brown evenly. Add the Lemon Balm and roast for another 5-10 minutes. Check with fork to make certain Potatoes are tender.

Place Vegetables around Chicken after you have placed on serving platter.

CHOCOLATE MOUSSE TORTE WITH ORANGE SCENTED CRÈME ANGLAISE

MAKES 6 SERVINGS
I like to make this in a 9 inch loaf pan. You can also make it in a bowl. It comes out of either nicely and both are good presentations. You will need a double boiler and a hand mixer.

1- In small sauce pan add Rum and Water and bring to a boil. Turn off and let cool to the touch.

2- Coat a 9 inch loaf pan with spray Oil.

3- Take Lady Fingers and gently dip into Rum Syrup and begin to line your pan with the rounded side of the Lady Fingers down. The bottom and sides should be covered with Lady Fingers. There can be slight gaps. You may have to cut some to do the best job.

4- Reserve the Syrup and Lady Fingers to put a top on the Chocolate Mousse after you fill the mold.

To Make the Mousse

1- In double boiler melt Chocolate, Coffee and Butter. Add Grated Orange Peel.

2- Put Egg Yolks and Sugar into small bowl and mix on medium speed until Yolks are pale yellow or ribbon stage.

3- Add the Yolk mixture to Chocolate mixture and continue to cook. Stir frequently over medium heat in double boiler, about 12-15 minutes. Remove from heat and transfer to another bowl. Let cool down for 10 minutes.

4- Beat the Egg Whites until they are stiff but not dry. Gently fold in the Egg Whites (a rubber spatula is the essential tool when doing this). Fold gently, you want the air to stay in the whipped Egg Whites to make the Mousse light.

5- Pour Chocolate Mousse into mold. Dip Lady Fingers into Rum Syrup and top the Mousse to complete the Mousse Torte.

6- Lightly cover with plastic wrap and refrigerate for at least four hours before serving.

7- When ready to serve use a knife and gently loosen the Torte from the mold. Tap the sides to make sure it is loose. Turn out upside down on serving dish.

8- Slice and place on dessert plate or shallow dessert bowl. Pour Crème Anglaise on the side of each slice.

Ingredients for Chocolate Mousse Torte

- 2   3 oz pkgs. Lady Fingers
- 2 tbls.   Rum
- 3 tbls.   Sugar
- 1/2 cup   Water

Ingredients for Chocolate Mousse Filling

- 8 oz.   Dark Sweet Chocolate
- 1 tbls.   Strong Coffee
- 1/4 lb.   Butter
- 3   Eggs (separated)
- 3/4 cup   Sugar
- 1 teas.   Grated Orange peel

Ingredients for Orange Crème Anglaise

- 5   Egg Yolks
- 1/2 cup   Sugar
- 1/2 cup   Cream
- 1/2 cup   Milk
- 3 pieces   Orange Peel

To Make Crème Anglaise

1- Put Egg Yolks and Sugar into small bowl and mix on medium speed until Yolks are pale yellow or ribbon stage.

2- In double boiler heat Cream, Milk and Orange Peel.

3- Add Egg Yolk mixture, stirring with a wire whisk. Cook for another 12-14 minutes to thicken.

4- Strain and cool. Serve with Chocolate Mousse Torte.

Lunch in the Garden

Menu

White Sangria

Crab Cakes
with Roasted Corn & Onion Relish

Grilled Potato & Scallion Salad
with Oil & Vinegar

Pan Seared Skate
in Mustard Sauce

Lemon Tart
with Lavender Whipped Cream
Candied Violets

CRAB CAKES WITH CORN & ONION RELISH

MAKES 6 SERVINGS
1 dozen Crab Cakes.

1- In large mixing bowl, beat Egg and blend with Dijon, Worcestershire, Green Onions, and Jalapeno Tartar Sauce. Stir until all ingredients are combined. *I often serve my Crab Cakes with my Jalapeno Tartar Sauce as a topping.*

2- Add Bread Crumbs and mix in before adding the Crab. You want to keep the Lump Crab Meat as whole as possible.

3- Using a biscuit cutter, mold the Crab Cake. You need to press it down to mold together in a nice uniform patty. Using a biscuit cutter to help shape it makes it look nice and holds together better than if you hand mold.

4- Have skillet pre-heated before adding 1 tbls. of Clarified Butter to 1 tbls. of Olive Oil at a time to brown Crab Cakes.

5- Brown Crab Cakes on both sides, then place on baking sheet to finish in the oven. Bake at 350 degrees for 10-12 minutes, then serve.

To make Corn and Onion Relish

1- Heat skillet over medium heat.

2- Mince White Onion and add to skillet, cook until they are caramelized, about six minutes, then add the minced Jalapeño and cook for another four minutes.

3- Add Fresh Corn Kernels, Garlic, White Balsamic Vinegar and Sugar.

4- Stir and cook for about five minutes. The Corn should be cooked but firm.

Ingredients for Crab Cakes		
•	1 lb.	Lump Crab Meat
•	1 cup	Japanese Bread Crumbs
•	1	Egg
•	2 teas.	Dijon Mustard
•	2 teas.	Worcestershire Sauce
•	1/4 cup	Minced Green Onion
•	1/2 cup	Jalapeno Tartar Sauce (recipe on page 103)

Clarified Butter & Olive Oil

Ingredients for Corn Relish		
•	1/2 cup	Minced White Onion
•	1 teas.	Minced Red Jalapeno
•	1 cup	Fresh Corn
•	1 clove	Roasted Garlic
•	1 tbls.	White Balsamic Vinegar
•	2 tbls.	Sugar

Pan Seared Skate in Mustard Sauce

Skate or Ray Wings can be used in this dish. West Coast Fishermen catch Big Skate and California Skate. East Coast Fishermen catch Butterfly Ray and Winter Skate. You can purchase skinned filets from a good Fish Shop. Skate Wings are often cut out to look like large Sea Scallops because the texture and taste is similar to Scallops. If you live in an area that you can't find this fish, Catfish filets are a fine substitute as well as Halibut or Sea Bass.

MAKES 6 SERVINGS

1- Cut Fish Filets into twelve 4 oz. or six 8 oz. portions. Season Fish Filets with a mixture of the Salt, Garlic and Pepper.

2- Place Flour in a pie tin or plate. Lightly dust each Fish Filet in Flour.

3- Put sauté pan or cast iron skillet over high heat. Add 1 tbls. of Butter per 8 oz. of Fish. Let Butter melt, but place Fish Filet in pan before Butter browns. Cook Fish by browning on both sides. Remove Fish into an oven proof serving dish.

4- After browning all the Fish Filets, keep the pan over medium heat. Add the Shallots and stir in the hot pan until the Shallots are browned.

5- Add the Mustard, White Wine and Cream. Stir and let simmer for 4 to 5 minutes. The Sauce should reduce by nearly half.

6- With wire whisk, add softened Butter a tablespoon at a time. You should have a Creamy Mustard Sauce.

7- Put oven proof serving dish containing the browned Fish Filets into 375 degree oven for ten minutes.

8- Spoon Sauce over Fish evenly. Heat for another five minutes and serve immediately.

Ingredients for Skate Wings in Mustard Sauce

•	3 lbs.	Skate Filet
•	1/2 cup	Flour
•	1/2 teas.	Salt
•	1/4 teas.	Garlic Powder
•	1/4 teas.	Black Pepper
•	1/4 lb.	Butter

Ingredients for Mustard Sauce

•	2 tbls.	Minced Shallots
•	4 tbls.	Grain Mustard
•	1/4 cup	White Wine
•	1/2 cup	Cream
•	4 tbls.	Soft Butter

Grilled Potato Salad

Ingredients for Grilled Potato Salad with Scallions

•	2 lbs.	Small New Red Potatoes
•	1/4 cup	Balsamic Vinegar
•	1/4 cup	Olive Oil
•	1 teas.	Salt
•	1 tbls.	Sugar
•	1/4 teas.	Black Pepper
•	1 bunch	Green Onions

Optional

•	1 Cup	Kalmata Olives

MAKES 6 SERVINGS

1- Boil New Red Potatoes until tender. Strain and rinse with cold water. Cut each Potato in half.

2- In large mixing bowl add Balsamic Vinegar, Olive Oil, Salt, Sugar and Pepper. Mix together and add Potatoes. Toss Potatoes in Vinegar mixture.

3- On hot charcoal grill, grill Potatoes on all sides. Put Potatoes back in Vinegar mixture.

4- Dice Green Onions (top and the white bulb). Add to Grilled Potatoes and toss.

LAVENDER WHIPPED CREAM

MAKES 1 CUP

1- In cold metal bowl add Cream. With wire whisk, electric whisk or beaters, whip Cream until soft.

2- Slowly add in Sugar and Lavender Oil. Continue to whip into soft peaks. You don't want the Cream too stiff.

Tea Cake Crust
You will need a 9 inch tart pan. You can use a traditional pie crust if you like. I prefer to make this tart with the Southern Tea Cake recipe as a crust. It makes this Lemon Tart much richer and better than the traditional ones. That recipe is on page 66. You roll it out and line the pan just as you would with any pie dough. Chill the tart pan with the Crust in it for 15 minutes. Then pre-bake before filling with Lemon Custard. Bake at 350 degrees for 15-18 minutes until golden brown.

Ingredients for Lavender Whipped Cream

- 1/2 pint — Whipping Cream
- 2 tbls. — Extra Fine Sugar
- 3 drops — Lavender Oil

Ingredients for Lemon Tart Filling

- 1 cup — Sugar
- 3 tbls. — Flour
- 3 tbls. — Corn Starch
- 1/2 teas. — Salt
- 1 1/2 cups — Boiling Water
- 2 — Egg Yolks
- 1/2 cup — Fresh Lemon Juice
- 2 teas. — Grated Lemon Rind
- 3 tbls. — Butter
- 3 tbls. — Candied Violets

LEMON TART WITH TEA CAKE CRUST

MAKES 1 PIE OR 6 SERVINGS

You will need a double boiler or you can use a metal bowl that fits into a pan with water to create a double boiler. With a double boiler the water in the bottom pan should be brought to a boil, then turned down to a simmer for best results. The idea behind using a double boiler is to not cook a sauce or custard too fast, so it can thicken without burning or separating. Set up your double boiler first before you begin with the directions below.

1- Sift Sugar, Flour, Corn Starch and Salt together.

2- Put 1 1/2 cups Boiling Water in the top of the double boiler. Add the Sugar and Flour mixture, stirring to keep smooth. Cook while stirring almost constantly until it thickens, about 15 minutes.

3- Beat Egg Yolks for one minute before adding to thickened Sugar mixture. Add and cook for two more minutes. Add Lemon Juice and grated Lemon Rind. Whisk in Butter.

4- Remove Lemon Custard from the heat. Let cool for 10 minutes before pouring into baked tart shell.

5- Chill Tart before serving. Add a heaping tablespoon of Lavender Whipped Cream on each piece.

6- Garnish with Candied Violets or Fresh Lavender if available.

White Sangria

- 1.5 ML. WHITE WINE
- 1 CUP PEACH SCHNAPPS
- 2 ORANGES SLICE INTO ROUNDS AND CUT IN HALF AGAIN
- 2 LEMONS SLICE INTO ROUNDS AND CUT IN HALF AGAIN
- 2 PEACHES SLICED THIN

PUT INTO PUNCH BOWL AND ADD 1 QT. OF SMALL ICE CUBES RIGHT BEFORE SERVING.

SERVE IN PUNCH CUPS OR WINE GLASSES.

THIS IS A REFRESHING DRINK FOR A SUMMER LUNCHEON.

35

Until I had them in Paris Bistros I did not even know what I was missing. As much as I love French food,

in my cooking I always seem to add a touch of the South. The smoky, spicy Andouille Sausage with a touch of Jalapeno makes the taste of this Mussel dish even more memorable. In the South the Spring is the best time to dine outside no matter what you serve. If you don't feel like making this entire menu you can serve the Mussels with Crusty French Bread and make a simple meal of just the Mussels and Bread. The Chicken Breast on Spinach or the Pasta in Tomato Cream can stand alone as satisfying meals. Just add a Salad and Bread.

Bistro Supper on The Patio

Menu

Mussels with Andouille
Jalapeno-Basil Broth

Poached Chicken Breast
on a bed of
Fresh Spinach
with
Anchovy, Lemon & Garlic

Penne Pasta with Spicy
Tomato Cream

Chocolate-Hazelnut
Pot de Crème

MUSSELS IN
ANDOUILLE JALAPENO-BASIL BROTH

MAKES 6 SERVINGS
This is for an appetizer, for an entrée this recipe makes 3 servings. You will need a large sauté pan with a lid.

1- Cut the Andouille Sausage into a small 1/4 inch dice. Mince the Garlic. Cut the Jalapenos into thin strips, removing the seeds. You may want to wear rubber gloves when handling Jalapenos or be careful and wash your hands well after handling the Peppers. The seeds of the Peppers hold 80% of the capsaicin (or hotness).

2- Heat the sauté pan over high heat. When the pan gets hot add the Andouille Sausage. The Sausage has enough fat in it that you do not need to oil the pan. Brown the Andouille. Add the Garlic and Jalapenos. Sauté for a few seconds.

3- Add the cleaned Fresh Mussels. Sauté for about 30 seconds. Add the Wine. Cook for 3 minutes. Add the Water. Cook for 1 minute.

4- Add the Basil and Salt. Cover with the lid and simmer for 5 minutes. Let stand for another 5 minutes before serving.
You can hold this dish for 30 minutes before serving. It is still very good at room temperature.

Ingredients for Mussels in Andouille Jalapeno-Basil Broth		
•	1/2 lb.	Andouille Sausage Links
•	6 cloves	Minced Garlic
•	1 or 2	Fresh Jalapenos
•	3 lbs.	Black or Green Lip Mussels
•	1/2 cup	Dry White Wine
•	1/2 cup	Water
•	2 tbls.	Julienne Fresh Basil
•	1/4 teas.	Sea Salt

Ingredients for Garlic Bread		
•	1 loaf	French Baguette
•	3 tbls.	Butter
•	1 tbls.	Mayonnaise
•	1 tbls.	Minced Garlic
•	1/4 teas.	Minced Parsley
Optional		
•	3 tbls.	Grated Parmesan

CREAMY GARLIC BREAD

MAKES 6 SERVINGS

1- Cut Baguette into 1/2 inch rounds. Lay on baking sheet.

2- Soften Butter. In food processor, blend Butter, Mayonnaise and Garlic.

3- Add minced Parsley by hand.

4- Spread on Baguette Rounds and toast in 400 degree oven for 7-8 minutes.

Sprinkle with Parmesan for a variation.

POACHED CHICKEN BREAST
ON A BED OF FRESH SPINACH
WITH ANCHOVY, LEMON & GARLIC

MAKES 6 SERVINGS
To Poach the Chicken

1- Dice Carrot into 1/2 inch pieces, quarter Shallots.

2- Heat a large 12 inch sauté pan, add Carrots and Shallots to roast for 1 minute, then add the White Wine and reduce in half.

3- Add Water, Salt and Pepper Flakes to sauté pan. Simmer for two minutes.

4- Add Chicken Breasts and cover with lid. Cook until Breasts are firm to touch and cooked all the way through. Cooked Chicken Breasts should register 140 degrees on your meat thermometer.

To Sauté the Spinach

1- Slice Garlic Cloves length-wise into thin slices.

2- Put large sauté pan over medium heat.

3- When pan is hot add Olive Oil.

4- When Olive Oil is hot add Garlic slices.

5- Add Anchovy Filets, stir and mash with a fork.

6- Add Spinach Leaves, toss to coat with Garlic and Anchovy.

7- Add Lemon Juice.

To Serve
Place Spinach on platter with Chicken Breasts on top. Garnish Chicken Breast with a Lemon Slice and an Anchovy Filet on top. Sprinkle chopped fresh Parsley and serve.

Ingredients for Poached Chicken Breast		
•	1 med.	Carrot
•	2	Shallots
•	3 cups	Water
•	1 cup	White Wine
•	1/2 teas.	Salt
•	1/4 teas.	Red Pepper Flakes
•	6 each	8 oz. Boneless Skinless Chicken Breasts

Ingredients for Sautéed Spinach		
•	1 tbls.	Olive Oil
•	1	Fresh Lemon
•	6	Garlic Cloves
•	3	Anchovy Filets
•	1 1/2 lbs.	Fresh Baby Spinach

Ingredients for Garnish		
•	6	Lemon Slices
•	6	Anchovy Filets
•	3 teas.	Chopped Fresh Parsley

PENNE PASTA WITH SPICY TOMATO CREAM

MAKES 6 SERVINGS

1- In food processor, chop Carrot and Onion.

2- Place sauce pan over medium heat, when hot add Olive Oil, chopped Carrots and Onion. Cook until Carrots and Onion begin to soften and brown.

3- Add Garlic, Green Onion and canned diced Tomatoes, cook for 15 minutes.

4- Add Cream, Crushed Red Pepper Flakes and Basil. Cook for another 15 minutes.

5- Cook Penne Pasta according to directions. Typically 10-12 minutes. Place hot Penne pasta in shallow pasta dish or bowl.

6- Pour half the Spicy Tomato Sauce on top and toss. Then pour the rest of the Sauce on top to serve.

If you want to do this dish ahead, after you add the first half of the Sauce - toss and refrigerate. Refrigerate the other half of the Sauce. When ready to serve add the other half of the Sauce to the Pasta, stir and microwave to reheat.

Ingredients for Penne Pasta with Spicy Tomato Cream

•	2 tbls.	Olive Oil
•	1/4 cup	Carrot
•	1/2 cup	Onion
•	2 teas.	Minced Garlic Cloves
•	1/4 cup	Minced Green Onion
•	2 cups	Diced Tomato in Juice
•	1/4 teas.	Crushed Red Pepper Flakes
•	3 tbls.	Fresh Basil
•	1/2 pint	Heavy Cream
•	4 cups	Cooked Penne Pasta
•		Salt to taste

CHOCOLATE HAZELNUT POT DE CRÈME

Ingredients for Chocolate-Hazelnut Pot de Crème

•	1 cup	Cream
•	2 tbls.	Half & Half
•	6 oz.	Chocolate Chips
•	3 each	Egg Yolks
•	1/2 cup	Hazelnuts (toasted)

MAKES 6 SERVINGS
You will need 6 Pot de Crème pots or 6 Demitasse cups.

1- In small sauce pan add Cream and Half & Half. Heat but do not boil.

2- In blender add Hazelnuts and puree to a powder. Loosen with a wooden spoon so they are not stuck to sides.

3- Add Chocolate Chips and puree with Hazelnuts.

4- Add warm Cream mixture to blender and blend until smooth.

5- Add Egg Yolks one at a time and blend well.

6- Pour into cups. Chill overnight and take out one hour before serving.

I love April because Oysters, Crawfish and Strawberries are abundant where I live.

April is one of my favorite months because some of my favorite foods are at their peak during this month. Most of my menus you could make a meal out of preparing just one of the recipes. I am sure by now you see my philosophy "more is better". There are so many good ways to prepare oysters that for many years on my menu at Regina's I had Oysters 2-2-2, several toppings that could be mixed and matched. To this day one of my favorites is the Eggplant and Bacon Dressing topped with Provolone Cheese.

Oyster Dinner
Menu

**Baked Oysters
in the shell
with Eggplant
& Bacon Dressing**

**Fried Crawfish with
Corn & Tomato Salad**

**Oyster Stew
with Salsa Verde**

**Butter Cake with
Louisiana Strawberries and
Grand Marnier Syrup**

BAKED OYSTERS WITH EGGPLANT & BACON DRESSING

MAKES 8 SERVINGS FOR APPETIZERS

1- Place heavy 3 qt. sauce pan over medium heat and add diced Bacon and cook until Bacon is crisp. Remove Bacon but leave Bacon drippings in to sauté vegetables.

2- Add Onion, Red Bell Pepper and Celery and sauté for 4-5 minutes until soft.

3- Add Eggplant and cook for another ten minutes or until Eggplant is soft.

4- Add Garlic, Thyme, Basil and Oregano and cook for 1 minute while stirring.

5- Stir in the Flour and mix well. Cook for another minute and slowly add the Cream.

6- Continue to cook until the Cream has begun to thicken.

7- Stir in the Bread Crumbs and cooked Bacon.

8- Top each Oyster with a generous portion of the Eggplant-Bacon Dressing.

9- Bake at 375 for 12 minutes.

10- Top with grated Provolone Cheese and continue to bake for another 6-8 minutes. Cheese should be slightly browned.

Ingredients for Baked Oysters

•	24	Shucked Oyster in the half Shell
•	4 slices	Smoked Bacon, Diced
•	1/2 cup	Diced Onion
•	1/4 cup	Diced Red Bell Pepper
•	1/4 cup	Diced Celery
•	3 cups	Peeled, Diced Eggplant
•	2 teas.	Minced Garlic
•	1/2 teas.	Thyme
•	1 teas.	Minced Basil
•	1/2 teas.	Oregano
•	2 tbls.	Flour
•	1/2 pint	Heavy Cream
•	1 cup	Italian flavored Bread Crumbs
•	2 cups	Grated Provolone Cheese

FRIED CRAWFISH FOR SALAD

MAKES 8 SERVINGS FOR SALAD

Heat Oil to 375 degrees

1- Drain Crawfish.

2- In medium bowl add Buttermilk and beat in 1 Egg.

3- Add 1 tbls. of Cajun Seasoning. Everyone has their favorite. Some are Salted heavier than others so just be aware.

4- Add Crawfish to Buttermilk mixture.

5- In another bowl add 1 tbls. of Cajun Seasoning to 4 cups of flour.

6- Drain the Crawfish and toss them in the flour mixture.

7- Separate them before dropping into cooking Oil.

8- Fry until golden brown. They should only take about 3-4 minutes to fry.

Ingredients for Fried Crawfish Tails

•	1 lb.	Crawfish Tails
•	1 cup	Buttermilk
•	1	Egg
•	4 cups	Flour
•	2 tbls.	Cajun Seasoning
•		Frying Oil

For fresh seafood, find a reliable source. Do not think twice about asking how fresh the product is. Be sure and tell your fish vendor how and when you are going to prepare their product. If you have any doubt your oysters, fish or shellfish are not fresh do not use them, return them right away to the source you purchased them.
With Seafood...better safe than sorry.

CORN & TOMATO SALAD

MAKES 8 SERVINGS

1- Place Mixed Greens on a platter. Keep chilled in refrigerator.

2- Get cast iron skillet very hot and roast fresh Corn Kernels until brown. Let cool before adding to Salad.

3- Cut Roma Tomatoes into quarters. While skillet is still hot, roast Tomatoes to give more flavor. Let cool before adding to Salad.

4- Julienne Red Onion into thin strips.

5- Arrange Tomatoes on top of Mixed Greens, then top with julienne of Red Onion and finish with Corn Kernels.

6- Keep chilled until ready to serve.

7- Drizzle with Remoulade Sauce.

8- Top with Fried Crawfish.

Ingredients for Corn and Tomato Salad		
•	1 lb.	Mixed Baby Greens
•	2 cups	Fresh Yellow Corn Kernels
•	6	Roma Tomatoes
•	1 med.	Red Onion

If you prefer a lighter Dressing you can use the Recipe for the Mustard Vinaigrette on page 148. Sometimes I toss the Greens in the Mustard Vinaigrette and drizzle a bit of Remoulade on the Fried Crawfish.

Ingredients for Remoulade Sauce		
•	4 tbls.	Creole Mustard
•	1/2 cup	Vinegar
•	1/4 cup	Catsup
•	2	Garlic Cloves
•	1/2 cup	Chopped Celery
•	1/2 cup	Chopped Green Onion
•	1 teas.	Paprika
•	1/4 teas.	Cayenne Pepper
•	1	Pasteurized Egg
•	1 cup	Salad Oil

REMOULADE SAUCE

MAKES 8 SERVINGS
This Remoulade Sauce will keep for one week in the refrigerator.

1- In blender add Creole Mustard, Vinegar, Catsup and blend.

2- Add Garlic, Celery and Green Onion then pulse until well blended.

3- Add Paprika, Cayenne Pepper and Egg. Blend for 30 seconds.

4- Slowly add Oil to emulsify.

5- Chill and use as Salad Dressing or Dip for Seafood.

OYSTER
STEW

MAKES 8 SERVINGS

1- Place heavy soup pot on low heat. Add Butter, melt slowly with out browning.

2- Add the Onions, Celery and Green Onions and cook for 10-12 minutes. Add Garlic for last minute.

3- Add fresh Basil and crushed Red Pepper Flakes.

4- Add the Flour and cook for two minutes to blend.

5- Add the Cream and simmer. The soup base should thicken. Add Half and Half and continue to simmer for 10 minutes.

6- Add the liquid from the Oysters and simmer.

7- Add the Oysters right before serving and cook for five minutes.

8- Serve within five minutes of cooking the Oysters.

In colder weather if I want to make this soup a bit heartier, I add Bacon and Potato. I dice four slices of Bacon and peel and dice two Potatoes. I cook the Bacon until cooked but not crisp. I remove it from the pan and then cook the Potatoes in the bacon fat. I add the Bacon and Potatoes right before I add the Oysters. This becomes more of a soup you can serve on its own.

Ingredients for Oyster Stew

- 1/4 lb   Butter
- 1/2 cup   Diced Onions
- 1/2 cup   Diced Celery
- 1 cup   Minced Green Onions
- 2 teas.   Fresh Minced Garlic
- 1 tbls.   Fresh Basil
- 1 teas.   Crushed Red Pepper Flakes
- 2 tbls.   Flour
- 1 pint   Cream
- 1 quart   Half and Half
- 1 quart   Oysters in liquid
-     Salt and Pepper to taste
- 1/2 cup   Sour Cream

Add 1 tbls. of Sour Cream to each bowl then top with Salsa Verde.

SALSA VERDE

If you are so inclined, I admit I often buy Mrs. Renfro's, it is as good as homemade.

Clean & blanch 1 lb. of fresh Tomatillos (do not cook, just blanch). Then puree in food processor.
1 medium Onion minced, sauté in Olive Oil and add the juice of one Lime and two tbls. of Cilantro and one minced Jalapeno. Cook for about three minutes, then add Tomatillo puree. You can make a large batch of this and can or freeze.

BUTTER CAKE
WITH FRESH STRAWBERRIES
AND GRAND MARNIER SYRUP

MAKES 8 SERVINGS

Preheat oven to 325 degrees. Grease and flour one 9 or 10 inch tube pan.

1- With an electric mixer, cream Butter and Sugar until fluffy. Add Eggs, one at a time and mix well.

2- Slowly add the Flour, one cup at a time while adding Cream a little at a time until all Flour and Cream is mixed in well.

3- Add the Vanilla, Orange Zest and Orange Extract and blend well. Pour batter into prepared pan.

4- Bake at 325 degrees for 1 hour and 20 minutes or until center springs back from small amount of pressure. Immediately turn out on cake rack to cool.

For Grand Marnier Syrup

1- In heavy sauce pan add all of the ingredients.

2- Turn on medium heat. Do not stir. Cook over medium heat for 8 minutes until Sugar begins to dissolve.

Ingredients for Cake and Syrup

- 1 cup   Butter
- 6   Eggs
- 3 cups   White Sugar
- 3 cups   Cake Flour
- 1 pint   Heavy Whipping Cream
- 1 tbls.   Vanilla Extract
- 2 tbls.   Grated Orange Rind
- 2 teas.   Orange Extract

1 Pint of Fresh Strawberries-wash and slice

- 1 1/2 cups   White Sugar
- 4 tbls.   Butter
- 2 teas.   Water
- 3 tbls.   Grand Marnier Liqueur

Louisiana Boiled Dinner

Menu

Spicy Boiled Shrimp
with Fresh Artichokes
Corn on the Cob
New Potatoes and Onions

Red Hot Cocktail Sauce
Caper Sauce

Avocado & Radish Salad
with Lime Vinaigrette

Calindas

SPICY BOILED SHRIMP WITH ARTICHOKES, CORN, POTATOES & ONIONS

MAKES 4 SERVINGS

Leave Shrimp shells on, but the Shrimp should be headless. If the heads are still on add another 1 lb. to the weight.

Have finger bowls ready with fresh Lemon and lots of napkins. It is messy, but a great Spring Dinner.

1- In large pot bring water to a boil. Cook New Potatoes for 10 minutes and remove.

2- Cut top of Artichoke blunt, then cut off stem. With scissors snip off tops of leaves. In same boiling water, cook Artichokes until a leaf pulls off easily or a fork goes through the bottom easily. Remove from water and cool. With a teaspoon scoop out the prickly center until you get to the bottom. Clean until the smooth Artichoke bottom is surrounded by larger size leaves.

3- In large pot put 5-6 qts. of water. Peel Pearl Onions, cut Lemons in half and add to water. Add Salt, Pickling Spice, Bay Leaves, Crushed Red Pepper and Cajun Seasoning. Bring to a boil. Boil for 10 minutes.

4- Add fresh Corn and New Potatoes and cook for another 5-7 minutes.

5- Add Shrimp and cleaned Artichokes and cook for 2 minutes and turn off heat. Let sit for 15 minutes.

6- Drain off excess water and serve on a large platter or tray.

*Serve with Cocktail Sauce and
Caper Sauce.*

Ingredients for Louisiana Style Boiled Shrimp Dinner

- 4   Medium Artichokes
- 8   New Potatoes
- 8   Pearl Onions
- 3   Lemons
- 2 lbs.   Large Gulf Shrimp
- 4   Ears of Yellow Corn

Ingredients for Spice Mixture for Shrimp Boil for 1 gallon of Water

- 2 tbls.   Kosher Salt
- 3 tbls.   Pickling Spice
- 6   Bay Leaves
- 3 tbls.   Cajun Seasoning

RED HOT COCKTAIL SAUCE

MAKES 1 1/2 CUPS
This will keep for two weeks in the refrigerator.

1- In small mixing bowl mix together the Catsup, Horseradish, Lea & Perrins, Fresh Lemon Juice and Franks Hot Sauce.
You may substitute any Worcestershire Sauce and any Red Hot Pepper Sauce.

Ingredients for Red Hot Cocktail Sauce		
•	1 cup	Catsup
•	3 tbls.	Horseradish
•	1 tbls.	Lea & Perrins
•	2 tbls.	Fresh Lemon Juice
•	1 tbls.	Franks Hot Sauce

CAPER SAUCE

Ingredients for Caper Sauce		
•	1 cup	Mayonnaise
•	2 teas.	Fresh Lemon Juice
•	2 tbls.	Dijon Mustard
•	2 tbls.	Capers
•	1/2 teas.	Fresh ground White Pepper

MAKES 1 1/4 CUPS

1-In serving bowl mix Mayonnaise, Lemon Juice, Dijon Mustard and Capers. Add fresh ground White Pepper. Stir and chill to serve.

LIME VINAIGRETTE

Ingredients for Lime Vinaigrette		
•	1	Small Shallot
•	1/4 cup	Fresh Lime Juice
•	1 tbls.	Fresh Lime Zest
•	1 tbls.	Orange Juice
•	1/2 cup	Salad Oil
•	1/2 teas.	Salt
•	1 tbls.	Sugar

MAKES 1 CUP

1- In blender add Shallot and Lime Juice, puree.

2- Add Lime Zest, Orange Juice, Salt, Sugar and slowly add Oil while blender is on.

Avocado-Radish Salad

MAKES 8 SERVINGS

1- Wash & dry 2 heads of Butter Lettuce.

2- Tear Butter Lettuce and place on 8 individual plates or one serving platter.

3- Peel Avocado and cut in half pulling a whole half away from the seed. Then slice Avocado and put one half of sliced Avocado on each Salad.

4- Slice Radishes and Red Onion very thin and evenly distribute over the Salad.

5- Drizzle Lime Vinaigrette over Salad and serve.

Ingredients for Avocado-Radish Salad		
•	4	Ripe Avocados
•	1 dozen	Red Radish
•	1/2 cup	Julienne Red Onion
•	2 heads	Butter Lettuce
•	1 cup	Lime Vinaigrette

Calindas
(Meringue Kisses)

Ingredients for Calindas		
•	2	Egg Whites
•	2 cups	Powdered Sugar
•	1 teas.	Cider Vinegar
•	1 teas.	Vanilla
•	1 cup	Finely Chopped Pecans
Optional-		
•	1 cup	Finely Chopped Dried Apricots
		Or Dried Cherries

Dried Cherries may be substituted for Apricots.

MAKES 2 DOZEN COOKIES
You will need two cookie sheets.
Preheat oven to 200 degrees.
Preheat oven to 200°

1- Line baking sheet with parchment paper.

2- In a bowl with an electric mixer beat Egg Whites until they hold soft peaks.

3- Gradually add Sugar, beating, and beat until meringue holds stiff, glossy peaks.

4- Add Vinegar and Vanilla, then fold in Pecans.

5- Drop heaping teaspoons of meringue about 1 inch apart onto baking sheet and bake in middle of oven 45 minutes.

6- Turn oven off and leave meringues in oven 1 hour or even 2 hours more.

7- With a metal spatula transfer meringues to a rack to cool completely before you put into an airtight container.

Afternoon Dessert Party
Menu

Coffee Bar
with Assorted Cordials

Dessert Wines

Lemon Squares   Fresh Fig Topping
Cinnamon Cake   Peach Topping

German Chocolate Squares
White Chocolate Sauce
Dark Chocolate Sauce

Homemade Vanilla Ice Cream

SETTING UP A COFFEE BAR

SERVES 24

When setting up for your party find a place on your patio or in your house that you can make your Coffee Bar a focus and easy for guests to get to.
You will need:

24 Coffee Cups & 24 teaspoons or demitasse spoons, a serving spoon for the Whipped Cream and a sugar spoon for the Cinnamon Sugar, sugar tongs for the Sugar Cubes.

A pretty Coffee Urn (party rental suppliers have these if you don't own one). Two decorative Sugar Bowls, one for the Sugar Cubes and one for the Cinnamon Sugar.

Tia Maria- a Coffee Liqueur from Jamaica.

Cognac- a Brandy distilled from a fermented mash of grapes. This fine Brandy is produced in the Cognac region of France. Remember all Cognac is Brandy but not all Brandy is Cognac.

Grand Marnier- an Orange Brandy which also goes well with Coffee and Chocolate.

There are numerous other Liqueurs that will work, it is a matter of personal preference and taste.

1- Whip Cream to soft peaks and put in decorative serving bowl. Keep refrigerated until ready to serve.

2- Make Cinnamon Sugar by mixing two tbls. of Sugar with Cinnamon. Put in decorative sugar bowl.

3- You can arrange the bottles on your coffee bar or you can pre-pour Liqueur into the Chocolate Cups. Keep your Chocolate Cups in a cool place until ready to serve.

4- Set up your Coffee to brew, but brew just in time to serve. Coffee is best when served within 15 minutes of brewing.

Ingredients for a Coffee Bar		
•	1 qt.	Whipping Cream
•	1 cup	Sugar Cubes
•	1 cup	Granulated Sugar
•	2 tbls.	Cinnamon
•	2 dozen	Chocolate Liqueur Cups
•	1 btl.	Tia Maria
•	1 btl.	Cognac
•	1 btl.	Grand Marnier
•	1 gal.	Fresh Brewed Coffee

DESSERT WINES

Dessert Wines are wonderful, but sweet. You are safe to plan on 4 oz. per guest. The combination of the Sugar content of the Wine and that it is well chilled is quite satisfying and is like having another Dessert.

Late Harvest Wines- when overly ripe grapes develop a good mold (Botrytis Cinerea) they lose moisture and their natural sugars become concentrated. This is what makes a Late Harvest Dessert Wine.

Fortified Wines- Port and Sherry are also classified as Dessert Wines. Fortified wines are made by adding "Grape Brandy" to Wine. Port is sweet because Brandy is added during fermentation, where Sherry is fortified after fermentation.

HOMEMADE VANILLA ICE CREAM

MAKES 2 QUARTS
The better quality your Vanilla, the better your Ice Cream.

1- In large metal mixing bowl add Egg Yolks, beat until foamy.

2- Add Sugar and beat until ribbon stage or pale yellow.

3- In sauce pan add Vanilla Bean and Half & Half. Let sit for 15 minutes to absorb some of the Vanilla. After 15 minutes bring the Half & Half to a simmer. Let stand for 5 minutes.

4- Slowly pour heated Half & Half into Egg and Sugar mixture, stirring with a whisk the whole time.

5- Set up a double boiler that you can sit your large metal mixing bowl over. Place metal bowl with Half & Half and Egg and Sugar mixture over double boiler and cook to a custard stage. This takes 12-15 minutes. Add Vanilla Extract.

6- Chill Custard very well. The Custard should be very cold before placing in your Ice Cream churn.

7- Whip Cream to soft peaks.

8- Remove Vanilla Bean from Custard and fold in Whipped Cream.

9- Follow the directions of your Ice Cream freezer.

I would make the Ice Cream very early in the day or, even better, the day before your party.

Helpful Notes-

Too much Water or Alcohol will make Ice Cream granular.

Too little Sugar or Fat (from the Milk) will also make the Ice Cream granular.

Be sure your Ice Cream churn scrapes the sides well.

Do not freeze too fast.

Ingredients for Vanilla Ice Cream	
• 16	Egg Yolks
• 1 1/2 cups	Sugar
• 1 qt.	Half & Half
• 1 pint	Heavy Cream
• 1	Vanilla Bean
• 2 tbls.	Vanilla Extract

Variations-

Banana Walnut Ice Cream- peel and mash 6 Bananas with 2 tbls. of fresh Orange Juice. Add to the Custard after Custard has cooled. Add 1 cup of chopped Walnuts to Whipped Ice Cream.

Black & White Ice Cream- 2 cups of Dark Sweet Chocolate Chips and 1 cup of White Chocolate Chips. Fold into the Whipped Ice Cream.

Fig with Lemon Zest- 2 pints of chopped Figs with 3 tbls. of Lemon Zest and one cup of Confectioners Sugar. Fold into Whipped Ice Cream.

Mint Chip Ice Cream- substitute Peppermint Extract for the Vanilla Extract. Add a few drops of green or pink food coloring. Fold 2 cups of Chocolate Chips into Whipped Ice Cream.

LEMON SQUARES

MAKES 8 SERVINGS
You will need a 9x13 cake pan or Pyrex dish. Spray with Vegetable Oil.

1- In mixing bowl add Condensed Milk with Lemon Juice and Lemon Rind. Set aside.

2- In food processor add Flour, Oatmeal, Baking Powder and Brown Sugar. Pulse to mix.

3- Cut chilled Butter into 6 or 8 pieces. Add and use pulse key on your processor. Do not over mix. Mixture should be crumbly.

4- Pour half of the Flour mixture into baking pan. Lightly press and bake for 5 minutes in a 350 degree oven.

5- Pour Lemon mixture into baking pan. Top with the rest of the Flour mixture.

6- Bake at 350 degrees for 25 minutes.

Cool and cut into any size squares you like.

Ingredients for Lemon Squares

- 15 oz.   Condensed Milk
- 1/2 cup   Fresh Lemon Juice
- 1 teas.   Lemon Rind
- 1 1/2 cups   Flour
- 1 cup   Oatmeal
- 1 teas.   Baking Powder
- 2/3 cup   Butter (1&1/2 sticks)
- 1 cup   Brown Sugar

Ingredients for Fresh Fig Topping

- 2 pints   Fresh Figs
- 1   Lemon
- 1 cup   Powdered Sugar

Ingredients for Fig Whipped Cream

- 1/4 cup   Fig Preserves
- 1 pint   Whipped Cream

FRESH FIG TOPPING

MAKES 8 SERVINGS

To make Fresh Fig Topping

1- Rinse and dry fresh Figs. Cut into quarters.

2- Zest the skin of the Lemon, then squeeze the Juice from the Lemon.

3- Toss the Fig quarters in the Powdered Sugar, Lemon Juice and add Lemon Zest and chill.

To make Fig Whipped Cream

1- In food processor puree Fig Preserves and chill.

2- Whip Cream until firm peaks form, then fold in Fig puree.

GERMAN CHOCOLATE SQUARES
WITH WHITE & DARK CHOCOLATE SAUCES

MAKES 8 SERVINGS
You will need a greased 9x13 inch baking pan.

Chocolate Squares
1- In sauce pan melt Butter and Chocolate.

2- In metal or glass bowl add Sugar, then pour in melted Chocolate and mix.

3- Mix in Eggs with a hand wire whisk. Do not over mix, but make sure Eggs are blended in well.

4- Add Flour with wire whisk. Once again, do not over mix.

5- Pour into greased baking pan. Bake at 350 degrees for 20-25 minutes.

German Chocolate Topping
1- In medium sauce pan add Butter and melt over medium heat. Add Cream.

2- Pour Sugar into mixing bowl and add Egg Yolks. Beat until pale yellow. Add to heated Cream, stirring so it does not curdle.

3- Add Coconut and cook for 3-4 minutes until mixture begins to thicken. Add Pecans. Cool for 10 minutes and pour over Chocolate Squares.

4- Cut into any size you like and serve.

Chocolate Sauces
1- In two separate glass bowls put Dark Chocolate Chips in one and White Chocolate Chips in the other.

2- Pour one cup of Cream into each bowl.

3- Microwave each bowl for 30 seconds at a time and stir. Continue until Chocolate Chips are melted and you have a smooth Sauce.

Ingredients for Chocolate Squares

- 3/4 cup   Butter
- 6 oz.   Unsweetened Chocolate
- 2 cups   White Sugar
- 2   Eggs
- 1 1/2 cups   Flour

Ingredients for German Chocolate Topping

- 1/2 cup   Butter
- 1 cup   Sugar
- 3   Egg Yolks
- 1 cup   Heavy Cream
- 1 cup   Shredded Coconut
- 1 cup   Pecans

Ingredients for White Chocolate and Dark Chocolate Sauces

- 1 pint   Heavy Cream
- 2 cups   Dark Chocolate Chips
- 2 cups   White Chocolate Chips

Upside Down
Peach & Raspberry Cake

MAKES 8 SERVINGS
You will need a 9 inch spring form pan sprayed with a spray vegetable oil.

For Cake

1- Cream Butter and Sugar.

2- Add Eggs one at a time and beat on medium speed until well blended.

3- Sift Flour with Baking Powder.

4- Alternately fold Flour mixture into Butter mixture with the Buttermilk and Vanilla until you have a smooth Batter.

For Bottom of Cake

5- Melt 1/4 lb. of Butter in glass bowl in microwave. Add Brown Sugar and stir. Do not dissolve Brown Sugar.

6- In bottom of spring form pan add Butter and Sugar mixture.

7- Arrange Peaches in any pattern you like. Place Raspberries around Peaches.

8- Pour in Cake Batter. Bake at 350 degrees until you can insert tooth pick and have it come out clean. 50-60 minutes is the typical time.

9- Let the Cake cool for 10 minutes then turn the cake pan upside down onto a 12 inch cake plate. Let cool, then loosen the sides of the spring form pan. Remove the round sides of the pan, then gently lift off the bottom.

10- The Cake must be removed while it is still a bit warm. If the Sugar Coating on the bottom cools it will stick. If for some reason the Cake cools before you take it from the pan, just stick it back in a hot oven for 4-5 minutes then remove from pan.

Ingredients for Cake

- 1/4 lb.   Butter
- 1 1/2 cups   Brown Sugar
- 2 cups   Cake Flour
- 2 teas.   Baking Powder
- 1 teas.   Baking Soda
- 3   Eggs
- 1/2 cup   Buttermilk
- 1 teas.   Vanilla

Ingredients for Bottom of Cake

- 1/4 lb.   Melted Butter
- 1 cup   Brown Sugar
- 2 cups   Sliced Peaches
- 1 cup   Raspberries

If you have to use frozen Peaches or Berries, make certain they are thawed and excess liquid is drained before arranging in the bottom of the spring form pan.

CINNAMON CAKE

MAKES 8 SERVINGS
You will need a 10 inch Bundt Pan. Spray very well with Vegetable Oil and dust with Flour.

1- Sift Flour, Salt, Baking Powder, Baking Soda, Cinnamon and White and Brown Sugar.

2- Put sifted dry ingredients into mixing bowl of mixer. Add softened Butter, Buttermilk, Vanilla and Sour Cream. Mix until ingredients are blended, about 45 seconds.

3- Add Eggs one at a time, beating each one into mixture for 15-20 seconds.

4- After all the Eggs are beaten into mixture, scrape sides and beat for another 30 seconds.

5- Pour Batter into Bundt pan and bake at 350 degrees for 60 minutes.

6- Let cool for 10-12 minutes before removing from pan onto wire rack.

Serve with Cinnamon Peach Topping

Ingredients for Cinnamon Cake

•	3 cups	Flour
•	1/2 teas.	Salt
•	1 tbls.	Cinnamon
•	3 teas.	Baking Powder
•	1 teas.	Baking Soda
•	1 cup	White Sugar
•	1 cup	Brown Sugar
•	1 cup	Butter, softened
•	1 cup	Sour Cream
•	1 teas.	Vanilla
•	4	Eggs
•	1 cup	Buttermilk

Ingredients for Peach Topping

•	1/4 lb.	Butter
•	2 tbls.	Peach Schnapps
•	1 cup	Brown Sugar
•	1 teas.	Cinnamon
•	1 teas.	Lemon Juice
•	1/2 teas.	Grated Lemon
•	4	Large Fresh Peaches

PEACH TOPPING

MAKES 8 SERVINGS

1- Peel and slice Peaches.

2- In sauce pan melt Butter with Peach Schnapps.

3- Add Brown Sugar and cook to syrup stage.

4- Add Cinnamon and Lemon Juice and grated Lemon Peel.

5- Add sliced Peaches and remove from heat.

6- Chill or serve room temperature over a slice of Cinnamon Cake.

Tea at Twin Oaks

Menu

Assorted Teas
Champagne Cocktails

Open Face Tea Sandwiches
Roast Beef with
Horseradish Cream Cheese
Lox with Capers & Onion
Roquefort & Watercress
Cucumber with Shrimp

Southern Tea Cakes
Lemon and Raspberry

Petits Fours
with Raspberry
& Butter Cream Filling

I think Afternoon Tea is a grand idea.

Being in the restaurant business for so many years it was hard to find a typical meal time with the fact I was always working. I discovered Afternoon Tea at the Clift Hotel in San Francisco, directly across the street from my Restaurant. It was the perfect haven for me. I would settle at my favorite table in the Redwood Room and the staff there would prepare the perfect pot of Lapsang Souchong (a smoky tea that I adore) and they would always give me a few extra tea sandwiches instead of a scone. I never once tired of this afternoon ritual.

As much as I love entertaining Breakfast is not my time of day to entertain. I began doing Afternoon Tea at Twin Oaks on Saturdays to get out of preparing breakfast for my guests. I thought it was more than an even trade..

HOW TO MAKE A PERFECT POT OF TEA

You will need a tea pot for each tea, a water kettle and a tea strainer. You always want to use loose tea, not bags. Loose tea leaves are a much higher quality than the dust (or tiny leaves) found in tea bags. For a Southern Afternoon Tea you can serve just one Tea or an assortment. If you are serving just one Tea, I would recommend Darjeeling or Earl Grey, one that has more universal appeal.

1- You always want fresh water in your kettle before boiling. You don't want to over boil the water as it will lose its oxygen and the tea will be bitter and sometimes muddy. The best water to use is cold tap water.

2- Just before the water boils add a little to each pot. Swirl the water around to warm the pot. This will help the brewing process because it will help hold the heat when you add your boiling water to the tea leaves.

3- In warm tea pot put a rounded teaspoon of tea per person and one extra for the pot. Then pour boiling water to fill the pot.

4- Allow tea to stand and brew for 3-6 minutes. The larger the tea leaves the longer they need to brew. Stir the tea once before serving.

5- Put the tea strainer over the cup and pour. If you take Milk in your tea it should be put in the cup before the tea is poured.

6- If you have the luxury of extra tea pots it is best to strain the perfectly brewed tea into another warm pot. This way it does not over brew.

Recommended Teas

- **Darjeeling** *a distinctive floral bouquet, a delicate wine-like Muscatel flavor.*

- **Lapsang Souchong** *a strong, pungent tea with a very smoky flavor. Never add Milk to this tea. I first had this tea in Paris and when I taste it-I taste Paris. It is one of the most exotic of teas.*

- **Earl Grey** *a blend of large leaf China Tea, Darjeeling and Bergamot (a pear shaped Mediterranean citrus fruit).*

- **Jasmine** *a blend of large leaf, semi-fermented leaves scented with jasmine flowers. Very aromatic.*

- **Ceylon** *grown at high altitudes, which is the prime growing conditions for tea. This produces a bright golden tea. Quite palatable to most tastes.*

CHAMPAGNE COCKTAIL

Ingredients for Champagne Cocktail

1 Bottle of Dry California Champagne

You should buy a basic Brut Champagne because you are adding Sugar and Bitters to the Champagne. There are many in the range of $15-$25.

- 6 Sugar Cubes

- Angostura Bitters

MAKES 6 COCKTAILS

1- In the bottom of each Champagne Glass or Flute place one Sugar Cube.

2- On each Sugar Cube add two dashes of Angostura Bitters.

3- Pour Champagne into each glass and serve.

You can get approximately 6 cocktails from a bottle of Champagne.

OPEN FACE TEA SANDWICHES

ROAST BEEF WITH HORSERADISH CREAM CHEESE
LOX WITH CAPERS & ONION
ROQUEFORT & WATERCRESS
CUCUMBER WITH SHRIMP

MAKES 8 SERVINGS OR 36 TEA SANDWICHES

These can be made a day ahead, just wrap <u>very well</u> with plastic wrap and refrigerate. Take out 1/2 hour before serving. You will need a sharp knife and a 1 1/2 inch Round Canapé Cutter.

1- Let Cream Cheese get to room temperature, mix in Mayonnaise until smooth. Divide into three small bowls, 6 tbls. in two bowls and 8 tbls. in the third bowl.

2- In one bowl with 6 tbls. add 1 teas. of Horseradish. This will be used for the Roast Beef. In the second bowl with 6 tbls. add the Roquefort. This will be used for the Roquefort and Watercress. Leave the bowl with 8 tbls. plain. This will be used for the Lox and the Cucumber Shrimp.

3- On a clean work surface line up 8 slices of Bread. Spread the plain Cream Cheese on these slices.

4- Take 4 of these slices of Bread with the plain Cream Cheese mixture and neatly arrange the Lox. Trim the crust away with a sharp knife. Cut into 4 finger sandwiches. Garnish with Capers and thinly sliced Red Onion.

5- Take the other 4 slices of Bread with the plain Cream Cheese mixture and using the round canapé cutter cut three rounds out of each slice of Bread. Top each round with a Cucumber slice and then use a little of the left over Cream Cheese mixture to hold a Shrimp in place on top of the Cucumber.

6- Take 4 slices of Bread and spread the Horseradish Cream Cheese. Neatly arrange Roast Beef. Trim the crust away with a sharp knife. Cut into 4 finger sandwiches. Garnish with thin slices of Radish.

7- Take the last 4 slices of Bread and spread the Roquefort Cream Cheese. Using the round canapé cutter cut three rounds out of each slice of Bread. Garnish with a fresh sprig of Watercress.

		Ingredients for Assorted Tea Sandwiches
•	16 slices	Pullman Style White Bread
•	8 oz.	Cream Cheese
•	4 tbls.	Mayonnaise
•	1 teas.	Horseradish
•	2 tbls.	Roquefort Cheese
•	1 teas.	Capers
•	2 tbls.	Thinly Sliced Red Onion
•	12 each	Cucumber Slices
•	12 each	Red Radish Slices
•	6 sprigs	Watercress
•	12	Cooked Shrimp *medium size (24 shrimp to the pound) so you need 1/2 lb.*
•	1/4 lb.	Medium Rare Roast Beef sliced thin
•	1/4 lb.	Lox sliced

SOUTHERN TEA CAKES

MAKES 2 DOZEN TEA CAKES
You will need a cookie sheet, a cookie cutter and a pastry brush.

1- In mixing bowl, cream Margarine and Sugar, add the Egg and beat until blended in.

2- Sift Flour and Baking Powder together and blend into creamed Margarine mixture.

3- Add Vanilla and Lemon Peel.

4- Chill for at least 3 hours or overnight.

To Shape, Fill & Bake

1- On Floured surface roll Dough out to 1/8 inch, cut out 48 cookies.

2- Take 12 and put a teaspoon of Raspberry Jam in the center. Take another 12 and put a teaspoon of Lemon Curd in the center. Wet the pastry brush and brush the edges of each filled cookie and top with an unfilled cookie. Press to seal.

3- Bake at 350 degrees for 12 minutes. These keep well in an air tight container.

MAKES A 12x16 SHEET
You will need a sheet pan 12x16 and a pastry brush.
Preheat oven to 350 degrees.

To Make Cake

1- Spray pan with vegetable oil (Pam or spray Canola oil is fine).

2- Sift Flour, add Baking Powder and sift again.

3- Cream Sugar and Butter until fluffy, gradually add two whole Eggs and 2 Egg Whites. Beat until well incorporated, then add Vanilla.

4- Add sifted Flour and Milk alternately until you have a smooth batter. Do not over beat.

5- With rubber spatula spread Cake Batter to cover sheet pan.

6- Bake at 350 degrees for 25 minutes.

7- Let cool in pan for 15 minutes, then turn onto a sheet of wax paper to finish cooling. Freeze for one day or longer.

Ingredients for Southern Tea Cakes

•	1/4 lb.	Margarine
•	1 cup	Sugar
•	1	Egg
•	2 cups	Flour
•	2 teas.	Baking Powder
•	1 teas.	Vanilla
•	2 teas.	Grated Lemon Peel
•	1/2 cup	Raspberry Jam
•	1/2 cup	Robertson's Lemon Curd

BASIC WHITE CAKE FOR PETITS FOURS

Ingredients for Cake

•	2 cups	Cake Flour
•	3 teas.	Baking Powder
•	1/2 cup	Butter
•	1 1/2 cups	Sugar
•	2	Eggs
•	2	Egg Whites
•	1 teas.	Vanilla
•	2/3 cup	Milk

PETITS FOURS

MAKES 2 DOZEN PETITS FOURS

You definitely want to make the Cake a day or two ahead. Then make the actual Petits Fours a day or two ahead of your Tea. They are time consuming to make but worth the effort. I usually do these over a three day period. I make the Cake and freeze it, the next day I make the Butter Cream and roll the Marzipan and layer it and re-freeze, on the third day I glaze them and decorate. You have to work with frozen Cake to avoid any crumbs in your glaze.
You will need a sheet pan of 12x16 White Cake, a pastry brush, a double boiler, and a wire rack .

To Make Butter Cream Filling
1- In mixing bowl whip the Butter and the Margarine until fluffy and smooth.
2- Add Vanilla Extract and Water.
3- Gradually whip in Powdered Sugar until you have a fluffy Butter Cream.

To Roll Out Marzipan or use Raspberry Jam instead
1- On clean surface or a pastry cloth dust with Powdered Sugar. Roll Marzipan out into a 6 inch x 8 inch rectangle.

To Make Fondant Glaze
1- In double boiler add Karo Syrup and Warm Water and Almond Extract, keep over high heat.
2- Slowly whisk in the Powdered Sugar. Stir and cook until you have a smooth glaze, about 12 minutes. Heat to 225 degrees. Cool to 110 degrees to cover Petits Fours. Color to your liking. Pastels are traditional. I use white and gold dust

To Assemble Petits Fours
You want to work with frozen Cake. This way you avoid getting crumbs in your glaze and your finished product will look a lot more professional.
1- Cut frozen Cake in half, two 12 inch x 8 inch rectangles.
2- Spread 1 cup of Butter Cream on one of the layers.
3- Top the Butter Cream with the Marzipan Sheet. Then top the Marzipan with Raspberry.
4- Cut 24 each 2 inch rounds.
5- Using a dry pastry brush, brush away loose crumbs.
6- Refreeze while making the Fondant Glaze.
7- Take frozen Cake Rounds and place on a grated baking rack. This way the extra fondant can run off.
8- Pour the glaze over each one, using a circular motion. You want to cover as much of the Petites Four as possible. Leave on wire rack to let Fondant set. It should be a smooth glaze that covers the Cake square except for the bottom. *If you are putting in Paper or foil paper holders, you can be less of a perfectionist. The Paper will cover the sides.*
9- With spatula remove Petites Fours and place in paper cupcake holders.

Ingredients for

Marzipan-Raspberry layer

- **8.8 oz. Betty Crocker Marzipan**
  I like this brand because it is packaged as a rectangle and it is easy to roll out to the proper dimensions.

- 1 cup   Raspberry Jam

Ingredients for Butter Cream

- 8 tbls.   Butter
- 4 tbls.   Margarine
- 1 teas.   Vanilla Extract
- 2 cups   Powdered Sugar
- 2 teas.   Water

Ingredients for Fondant Glaze

- 1/2 cup   Karo Syrup
- 1/2 cup   Warm Water
- 2 lbs.   Powdered Sugar
- 1/4 lb.   Butter (unsalted)
- 3 teas.   Almond Extract

To Decorate Petits Fours

1- Take extra Butter Cream and color it to a nice pastel contrast color.

2- Put in pastry bag with a # 1 writing tip.

3- Decorate with dots or with a window-pane design or any simple design you feel comfortable with.

I often use Gold Dust from a Baking shop or leave them plain and put in pretty gold foil cups.

Summer at Twin Oaks

When we first moved into Twin Oaks every Wednesday I grilled hot dogs for my two boys and all of their friends. More than often the parents of their friends arrived as well. There is not much to this... but it was a great recipe for spending time with my boys and getting to know their friends. My boys may have outgrown this tradition but it is probably the best recipe I have ever created.

The Southern Table

Menu

Southern Fried Chicken

Vegetable Slaw
with Green Goddess Dressing

Baked Red Potato Salad
with Grain Mustard

Mustard Greens
with Pepper Vinegar

White Corn Sticks
with Honey Butter

Rhubarb-Apple Crisp

What surrounds the Sunday Fried Chicken has much to do with the Season and the garden. Southern cuisine is so much more than fried food, but the South is proud to accept fried food as their own and there is no apology for it. At the Southern table there will be no sauce on the side unless it is the extra gravy. The Southern table is abundant and aromatic. The Southern table has linen and seems naked without flowers. The only silent pause at the Southern table is the blessing of the food, after that the volume climbs with each course and by dessert time it is almost deafening. The Southern table is home to me.

If you want a lighter lunch, you often find a Roast Chicken or a Chicken Fricassee at the Southern Table. I use my Pepper Marinade recipe to Roast Chicken or on occasion I use the simple but excellent combination of Lemon, Garlic and Rosemary. If you Roast your Chicken instead of frying it, you can add your Red Potatoes directly to the pan for extra flavor for a Baked Potato Salad. Some of my happiest memories of growing up in Natchez was sitting at my parents table on a Sunday for a long lunch with friends and family.

Vegetable Slaw with Green Goddess Dressing

MAKES 2 1/2 CUPS OF SALAD DRESSING
It is more Dressing than you need but it keeps for a few days and is wonderful on sliced Tomatoes or any Green Salad.

1- In blender put Garlic, Salt, White Pepper, Dry Mustard, Anchovy Paste, Tarragon Vinegar and blend.

2- Add Green Onions and Parsley Tops and continue to blend.

3- Add Mayonnaise and Sour Cream and blend until you have a fairly smooth Dressing.

MAKES 8 SERVINGS
You can find the Broccoli Slaw and Red Cabbage preshredded and packaged near the packaged Lettuces and Cabbage Slaw in the grocery store or you can shred your own with the grate attachment of your food processor.

1- Julienne the Sweet Red Peppers by cutting the seeds out and slicing the Peppers length-wise into very thin strips.

2- In large salad bowl mix Broccoli Slaw, shredded Purple Cabbage and Sweet Red Peppers.

3- Add 1/4 cup of Green Goddess Dressing at a time. Toss and stir until you have the right consistency. I recommend 1 cup of Dressing for this amount of Slaw.

Ingredients for Green Goddess Dressing

•	1	Garlic Clove
•	1/2 teas.	Salt
•	1/2 teas.	White Pepper
•	1/2 teas.	Dry Mustard
•	2 tbls.	Anchovy Paste
•	3 tbls.	Tarragon Vinegar
•	1/3 cup	Green Onion
•	1/3 cup	Parsley Tops
•	1 cup	Mayonnaise
•	1/2 cup	Sour Cream

Ingredients for Vegetable Slaw

•	2 cups	Broccoli Slaw
•	2 cups	Purple Cabbage Slaw
•	2 each	Sweet Red Peppers

Ingredients for Baked Red Potato Salad

•	2 lbs.	Small New Red Potatoes
•	1 teas.	Salt
•	1/2 teas.	Garlic Powder
•	1/2 teas.	White Pepper
•	3 tbls.	Grain Mustard
•	1 cup	Heavy Cream
•	1/2 bunch	Green Onions

Baked Red Potato Salad

MAKES 8 SERVINGS

1- Spray Oil in 2 qt. baking dish. Thinly slice New Red Potatoes and layer in baking dish. Season with Salt, Garlic Powder and White Pepper.

2- In small bowl mix Mustard with Cream, blend well with a wire whisk. Dice Green Onions and add to Mustard and Cream. Pour over sliced Potatoes.

3- Cover with foil and bake at 375 degrees for one hour. Then uncover and bake for 10-15 minutes more. Test with a fork to make sure they are tender to the touch.

MUSTARD GREENS WITH PEPPER VINEGAR

MAKES 8 SERVINGS

Hot Pepper Vinegar (make at least 3 days in advance).
1- Heat White Vinegar with Salt until Salt is dissolved.
2- In clean decorative Vinegar Bottle, push Peppers into bottle. Use a wooden skewer if needed to push to the bottom. Try to put as many Peppers as possible.
3- Cover Peppers with Vinegar and Salt mixture. Let cool before putting the top on.
4- Let sit for at least three days before using. It gets better with time.

Mustard Greens
1- In 6 qt. pot add 3 qts. of water. Put over medium heat.
2- Dice Onion and add to hot water. Add Smoked Turkey Leg, Garlic Salt and Crushed Red Pepper. Cook over medium heat for 30 minutes.
3- Wash the Mustard Greens well. Pat dry and cut or tear into 4 inch pieces.
4- Add to Smoked Turkey stock and cook for 15 minutes. Turn off, but let Greens remain in the Stock.
5- Serve warm. *The Pepper Vinegar is optional. If you don't have time you can use Tabasco or Crystal Hot Sauce.*

Ingredients for Mustard Greens

- 1 — Smoked Turkey Leg
- 12 lbs. — Mustard Greens
- 1 — Medium Onion
- 2 teas. — Garlic Salt
- 1/4 teas. — Crushed Red Pepper

Ingredients for Pepper Vinegar in decorative Vinegar Bottle

- 8-12 — Hot Chili Peppers
- 1/2 cup — White Vinegar
- 1/2 teas. — Salt

SOUTHERN FRIED CHICKEN

MAKES 8 SERVINGS

1- Rinse Chicken in cold water. Do not dry.
2- Mix Salt, Garlic, Black and Cayenne Pepper together to make your seasoning Salt.
3- Take 2 tbls. of Salt mixture and season the Chicken. Toss to distribute the Seasoning. Cover with plastic wrap and place in refrigerator at least three hours before frying. Overnight is even better.
4- Add the leftover Seasoning mixture to the 3 cups of Self Rising Flour.
5- Put Oil in electric skillet or a cast iron skillet. Heat to 350 degrees. The Oil should fill the skillet half way.
6- Take each piece of Chicken and coat very well with Seasoned Flour. Add Chicken to the hot Oil. You should have an inch space in between each piece as you are frying. Turn pieces to brown evenly.
7- Use a meat thermometer to check for doneness. It is the best way because of the difference in weight of each piece. They all require different cooking times. The temperature should register 140 degrees on your thermometer.
8- Drain on paper bag or paper towels to remove excess Oil.
Serve hot or room temperature.

Ingredients for Southern Fried Chicken

- 16 pieces — Chicken
- 4 teas. — Salt
- 2 teas. — Garlic Powder
- 1 teas. — Black Pepper
- 1/4 teas. — Cayenne Pepper
- 3 cups — Self Rising Flour
- 1 qt. — Frying Oil

WHITE CORN STICKS WITH HONEY BUTTER

MAKES 8 SERVINGS

White Corn Sticks

1- Preheat oven to 375 degrees. Preheat Oiled cast iron corn stick pan or a 9 inch cast iron skillet.

2- In mixing bowl add Self Rising White Corn Meal and Flour.

3- Add melted Margarine, Buttermilk and beaten Egg. Stir until you have a smooth Batter.

4- Pour into heated pan and bake for 12 minutes.

5- Serve right out of the oven.

Honey Butter

1- In small glass bowl mix softened Butter with Honey.
2- Leave at room temperature and serve with Corn Sticks or Corn Bread.

Ingredients for White Corn Sticks

- 1 2/3 cups   Self Rising White Corn Meal
- 1/3 cup   Self Rising Flour
- 4 tbls.   Margarine (melted)
- 1 1/2 cups   Buttermilk
- 1   Egg (beaten)

Ingredients for Honey Butter

- 1/4 lb.   Soft Butter
- 2 tbls.   Honey

RHUBARB-APPLE CRISP

MAKES 10-12 SERVINGS
You will need a 9x13 baking dish.

Crisp

1- Cut Butter into 1 inch pieces, put in food processor.
2- Add Oats, Flour and Sugar, pulse until it is crumbly,
the Butter should be the size of Peas.
3- Add Almonds and pulse just two or three times to blend in.
4- In baking pan sprayed with Oil put half the Crisp mixture to line the bottom of the pan and bake at 350 degrees for 8 minutes.

Filling

1- In metal or glass mixing bowl add diced Rhubarb and Apples. Add Sugar, Corn Starch and Cinnamon. Using a large spoon toss and stir until all ingredients are blended evenly.
2- Pour into Crisp pan and top with the rest of the Crisp mixture.
3- Bake at 325 degrees for 50-60 minutes. The center should firm like the sides. You can touch to see.

I think it is good as is but it seems to be the American way to put Whipped Cream or Ice Cream on top of everything. So if you must, stick with Vanilla Ice Cream or plain Whipped Cream.

Ingredients for Rhubarb-Apple Crisp

Ingredients for Crisp

- 3/4 lb.   Butter
- 1 1/2 cups   Quick Oats
- 2 cups   Flour
- 2 cups   White Sugar
- 1 cup   Almonds

Ingredients for Filling

- 2 cups   Diced Rhubarb
- 1 cup   Diced Tart Apples
- 1 cup   Sugar
- 3 tbls.   Corn Starch
- 1 teas.   Cinnamon

Summer Barbeque

Menu

Butter Lettuce Salad
with Grapefruit, Avocado
& French Dressing

BBQ Country Style Ribs
& Chicken Breasts
with Mango BBQ Sauce

Potato Salad
with Buttermilk Dressing

Baked Beans
with Bacon & Molasses

Upside Down
Peach & Raspberry Cake

Butter Lettuce Salad with Grapefruit & Avocado

MAKES 8 SERVINGS

1- Wash and chill Butter Lettuce until crisp. Remove the stem from the bottom, then cut each Head into quarters.

2- Peel Grapefruit, cut into sections, then cut into bite size pieces.

3- Cut the Avocado in half and remove seed, then peel off the skin. Cut the Avocado into pieces the same size as the Grapefruit. Gently mix with the Grapefruit. The acid from the Grapefruit will help prevent discoloration.

4- Place a quarter of Butter Lettuce on each plate or all on one serving platter. Top with Avocado and Grapefruit then drizzle French Dressing over Salad.

Ingredients for Butter Lettuce Grapefruit and Avocado Salad

- 2   Heads of Butter Lettuce
- 1   Ruby Red Grapefruit
- 4   Ripe Avocados

French Dressing

MAKES 8 SERVINGS

1- In food processor or blender add Catsup, Cider Vinegar and Brown Sugar. Blend for a few seconds.

2- Add Honey, Onion Powder and Celery Salt. Blend for 15 seconds.

3- Turn on food processor and slowly add Salad Oil.

4- This Dressing should be creamy.

Variations on this Dressing to use for other Salads.

Add two tbls. of chopped crisp Bacon.

Add two tbls. of Crumbled Blue Cheese or Goat Cheese.

Add two tbls. of minced Dried Tomato.

Add two tbls. of minced Dried Apricot or Mango.

Ingredients for French Dressing

- 1/4 cup   Catsup
- 1/4 cup   Cider Vinegar
- 1/4 cup   Brown Sugar
- 2 tbls.   Honey
- 1/4 teas.   Onion Powder
- 1/2 teas.   Celery Salt
- 1/2 cup   Salad Oil

POTATO SALAD WITH BUTTERMILK DRESSING

MAKES 8 SERVINGS

1- Cut New Potatoes into quarters, place in large pot and cover with cold water. Bring to a boil and test with a fork. Cook until tender but not falling apart. Rinse with cold water and drain.

2- Mince Green Onions using the tops and the whites of the Onion.

3- In separate mixing bowl add Buttermilk, Mayonnaise, Celery Salt, Garlic Powder, Onion Powder, Dill Weed and minced Green Onions.

4- Toss Red Potatoes, Green Onions and Dressing all together and chill for at least two hours before serving.

Ingredients for Potato Salad with Buttermilk Dressing

- 16 each   Small Red New Potatoes
- 1 bunch   Green Onions

Ingredients for Buttermilk Dressing

- 1/2 cup   Buttermilk
- 1/2 cup   Mayonnaise
- 2 teas.   Celery Salt
- 1 teas.   Onion Powder
- 1 teas.   Garlic Powder
- 1/2 teas.   Dill Weed
- 1/4 cup   Minced Green Onion

BAKED BEANS WITH BACON & MOLASSES

MAKES 8 SERVINGS

1- In 5 qt. soup pot add dry White Beans and 3 qts. of water. Bring to a boil, then turn off. Let sit for one hour, then drain off water.

2- In large roaster or bean pot, put soaked Beans and cover with water and Port Wine.

3- Add diced uncooked Bacon, diced Onion, Molasses, Brown Sugar, Dry Mustard and Salt.

4- Bake at 300 degrees for 3-4 hours. The cooking time varies so much with different brands of White Beans. Every hour check water and stir well. You may need to add more water in the beginning.

5- Beans should be moist but not watery.

Ingredients for Baked Beans

- 2 1/2 cups   Dry White Beans
- 1 cup   Port Wine
- 1/2 lb.   Smoked Bacon
- 1 med.   Onion
- 1/2 cup   Molasses
- 1 cup   Brown Sugar
- 2 tbls.   Dry Mustard
- 2 teas.   Salt

BBQ
COUNTRY STYLE RIBS
& CHICKEN BREASTS

MAKES 8 SERVINGS

1- In small bowl mix together Garlic Salt, Pepper, Paprika and Brown Sugar.

2- Rinse the Pork Ribs and toss with half the Spice Rub. Rinse the Chicken Breasts and toss with the other half of the Spice Rub and refrigerate.

3- The coals on your grill should be white hot. Spread the coals so you have even heat.

4- It is best to turn your Meat every six minutes when grilling and always use a meat thermometer.

5- When Meat is about 110 degrees brush a thin coat of the Mango BBQ Sauce on each piece.

6- Remove when Meat is 140 degrees.

Ingredients for Country Style Ribs and Chicken Breasts	
16	Country Style Pork Ribs
8	Chicken Breasts (bone-in)
3 teas.	Garlic Salt
1 teas.	Black Pepper
1 teas.	Paprika
3 tbls.	Brown Sugar

Ingredients for Mango BBQ Sauce	
1 med.	Onion
3 cups	Brown Sugar
10 oz. jar	Chili Sauce
2 tbls.	Tomato Paste
1/4 cup	Worcestershire
1/4 cup	Cider Vinegar
1/4 cup	Molasses
3 each	Ripe Mangos

MANGO BBQ
SAUCE

MAKES 8 SERVINGS

1- In food processor puree Onion. In medium sauce pan add Onion, Brown Sugar, Chili Sauce, Tomato Paste, Worcestershire Sauce, Cider Vinegar and Molasses.

2- Place sauce pan over low heat for 15 minutes until Sugar begins to dissolve. Then cook over medium heat for another 20 minutes.

3- Peel Mangos and mince in food processor.

4- Add to sauce pan and cook for 10 minutes more.

This sauce keeps for 4-5 days in the refrigerator or it may be frozen.

Ladies Luncheon Buffet

Menu

Rum Daiquiris

Cucumber Salad
with Yogurt & Dill Dressing

Grilled Tuna Salad with
Green Beans, Diced Potato
& Nicoise Vinaigrette

Grilled Chicken Salad with
Roasted Peppers & Cashews

Tomato & Artichoke Salad with
Basil-Orange Vinaigrette

Summer Fruits
marinated with Peach Schnapps
and Fresh Mint

CUCUMBER SALAD WITH YOGURT & DILL DRESSING

MAKES 8 SERVINGS

1- Peel Cucumbers and cut length-wise. Using a spoon, scoop out seeds from each Cucumber half. Cut into 1/2 inch slices.

2- Peel Red Onion and cut in half. Cut into thin strips.

3- In glass or metal bowl, mix Yogurt with Sour Cream.

4- Add Lemon Juice, fresh Dill and Salt. Stir well.

5- Add Cucumbers and Onions and toss.

6- Chill for at least one hour before serving.

This is best served the same day.

Ingredients for Cucumber Salad with Yogurt & Dill Dressing

- 5   Cucumbers
- 1/2   Red Onion
- 3/4 cup   Yogurt
- 1/4 cup   Sour Cream
- 2 teas.   Fresh Lemon Juice
- 2 teas.   Fresh Dill
- 1/8 teas.   Salt

GRILLED TUNA SALAD WITH NICOISE VINAIGRETTE

Ingredients for Grilled Tuna Salad

- 2 lbs.   Fresh Yellow Fin Tuna
- 1/4 cup   Olive Oil
- 2 teas.   Minced Garlic
- 8   New Red Potatoes
- 1 lb.   Fresh Green Beans
- 1/2 cup   Olive Oil
- 1/4 cup   Balsamic Vinegar
- 2 tbls.   Minced Nicoise Olives
- 1 teas.   Sugar
- 1/4 teas.   Cracked Black Pepper
- 1/4 cup   Pitted Nicoise Olives

MAKES 8 SERVINGS

1- Get grill hot. Marinate Tuna in Minced Garlic and Olive Oil. Add a touch of Salt and Pepper.

2- Grill Tuna to a medium rare. Let cool.

3- Cut New Red Potatoes into 1 inch cubes. Boil until soft but firm.

4- Cook Green Beans in boiling water for 2 minutes. Drain and cool.

5- In bowl mix Olive Oil, Balsamic Vinegar, Minced Olives, Sugar and Black Pepper.

6- On serving platter or salad bowl arrange Potatoes, Green Beans and Nicoise Olives and break Tuna into one inch pieces. Drizzle with Olive Dressing.

GRILLED CHICKEN SALAD WITH ROASTED PEPPERS & CASHEWS

MAKES 8 SERVINGS

1- Season Chicken Breast with Salt and Pepper. Brush with Oil and grill. Cool and slice into 1/4 inch slices.

2- Arrange shredded Romaine on serving platter.

3- Top with Grilled Chicken slices, arrange Roasted Peppers around sliced Chicken.

4- Puree Mayonnaise with Roasted Peppers and spoon Roasted Red Pepper Mayonnaise in the center of the sliced Chicken.

5- Sprinkle Cashews on top and serve.

You may put Roasted Red Pepper Mayonnaise on the side or you may substitute a Vinaigrette.

Ingredients for Grilled Chicken Salad with Roasted Peppers & Cashews

- 4   7 oz. Boneless, Skinless Chicken Breasts
- 2   Roasted Red Peppers
- 1/4 cup   Roasted Salted Cashews
- 4 cups   Shredded Romaine
- 1/2 cup   Mayonnaise
- 1/4 cup   Roasted Red Pepper

Salt and Pepper to taste

TOMATO & ARTICHOKE SALAD

MAKES 8 SERVINGS

1- Cut Radicchio into quarters. In bowl mix Olive Oil, Garlic, Lemon Juice, Salt and Pepper. Toss Radicchio quarters in Oil mixture.

2- Grill Radicchio for just a minute or so. This is more for flavor more than for cooking.

3- Quarter Tomatoes and Artichoke Hearts.

4- On serving platter arrange Radicchio, pulling the leaves apart.

5- Top with quartered Artichoke Hearts and arrange quartered Tomatoes around Radicchio.

6- Drizzle Basil-Orange Vinaigrette over Salad and serve.

Ingredients for Tomato & Artichoke Salad

- 2 each   Radicchio
- 1/2 teas.   Minced Garlic
- 1/4 cup   Olive Oil
- 1 teas.   Fresh Lemon Juice
-    Salt & Pepper
- 4   Firm, Ripe Tomatoes
- 12   Artichoke Hearts
- 1/2 cup   Basil-Orange Vinaigrette (page 86)

BASIL-ORANGE VINAIGRETTE

MAKES 8 SERVINGS

1- In blender or food processor add Shallot and puree.

2- Add fresh Orange Juice, Lemon Juice, Salt and Sugar.

3- Blend for a few seconds.

4- While blender is going add Oil.

5- Add Orange Zest and Julienne Basil after you have turned off the blender or processor.

Ingredients for Basil-Orange Vinaigrette

- 1   Shallot
- 1/4 cup   Fresh Orange Juice
- 1 tbls.   Fresh Lemon Juice
- 1/2 cup   Salad Oil
- 1/2 teas.   Salt
- 1 tbls.   Sugar
- 1 tbls.   Zest of Fresh Orange
- 2 tbls.   Julienne Fresh Basil

SUMMER FRUITS MARINATED WITH PEACH SCHNAPPS & FRESH MINT

Ingredients for Summer Fruits in Peach Schnapps

- 1   ripe Cantaloupe
- 1   ripe Honey Dew
- 3   ripe Peaches
- 1 pint   Raspberries
- 1/2 cup   Peach Schnapps
- 1/2 cup   Sugar
- 3 tbls.   Julienne Fresh Mint

MAKES 8 SERVINGS

1- Cut Cantaloupe and Honey Dew melons in half. Scoop out seeds. Use a melon ball scoop and make balls from Melon. Save the Honey Dew melon shell to serve dessert in.

2- Peel and dice Peaches.

3- Mix Peach Schnapps and Sugar to make Syrup.

4- In bowl gently toss Melon Balls and Peaches. Add Peach Schnapps Syrup.

5- Gently add Raspberries, do not toss or the Raspberries will fade onto your other fruits.

6- Add Mint. Chill and serve in Honey Dew shells.

Recipe for Daiquiris

FOR 8 DAIQUIRIS
8 SUGAR RIMMED MARTINI GLASSES

- 1/2 CUP FRESH LEMON JUICE
- 1/2 CUP FRESH LIME JUICE
- 1/2 CUP OF SIMPLE SYRUP
- 1/2 CUP RUM

MIX ALL OF THE INGREDIENTS IN A PITCHER.
IN COCKTAIL SHAKER ADD 1/4 CUP PER DRINK AND LOTS OF ICE.
SHAKE VIGOROUSLY UNTIL ICE COLD AND POUR INTO A SUGAR RIMMED MARTINI GLASS.

Making Daiquiris with fresh lemon and lime is so worth the effort. If you need to take a short cut you can use frozen lemonade and mix frozen lime juice. You will have a decent drink but it will not compare to the real thing.

MANGO SHRIMP
MARTINI
RECIPE PAGE 90

Summer Cooking Class

Menu

Mango Shrimp Martinis

Pan Seared Salmon with
Molasses~Bacon Vinaigrette

Blackberry~Crème Brule Trifle

MANGO SHRIMP MARTINI

MAKES 8 Mango Shrimp Martini's
You will need 8 Martini Glasses

1- Peel & slice Mango and arrange 4 slices in each Martini glass to make a tulip design.

2- Put about a 1/3 cup of shredded Romaine Lettuce in each glass

3- In a bowl mix Lemon Juice, Red Onion, Minced Tomatoes, Capers, Horseradish, Catsup, Worcestershire Sauce and Skyy Vodka.

4- Spoon 1/4 cup of sauce into each Martini glass.

5- Top with Shrimp and serve chilled.

Pre-set these on the table before you seat your guests. It adds color and is a wonderful dish you can prepare hours before.

Ingredients for Mango Shrimp Martini

- 32   Large Shrimp
- 3 cups   Shredded Romaine
- 2   Ripe Mangos

Cocktail Sauce Ingredients

- 2 tbls.   Lemon Juice
- 1/2 cup   Minced Red Onion
- 3 cups   Finely Minced Tomatoes (Roma, Green & Yellow- at least two colors of tomato if possible)
- 4 tbls.   Capers
- 4 tbls.   Horseradish
- 1 cup   Catsup
- 2 tbls.   Worcestershire Sauce
- 3 oz.   Skyy Vodka (optional)

Ingredients for Salmon with Bacon-Molasses Vinaigrette

- 8 each   6-7 oz. Fresh Salmon Filets
- 2 teas.   Smoked Sea Salt
- 1 teas.   Cracked Black Pepper
- 4 slices Hickory Smoked Bacon- thick slice

Vinaigrette- Add the ingredients in a blender. Blend until smooth.

- 4 tbls.   Aged Balsamic Vinegar
- 2 tbls.   Molasses
- 1 teas.   Garlic
- 1 tbls.   Minced Shallot
- 1 tbls.   Chopped Basil
- 4 tbls.   Cracked Black Pepper
- 4 tbls.   Olive Oil

PAN SEARED SALMON WITH BACON-MOLASSES VINAIGRETTE

1- Season Salmon Filets with Smoked Sea Salt and cracked Black Pepper.

2- Dice and cook Bacon until crisp. Remove cooked Bacon and drain on a paper towel.

3- Let the Bacon grease get hot enough to sear the Salmon. Place Salmon top side down for 1 minute, then turn to other side. The Salmon should be crusty on the outside but moist on the inside. Continue this until you have the Salmon cooked to your liking. Three minutes is usually perfect.

Place Salmon on greens, drizzle Vinaigrette and garnish with crisp Bacon.

BLACKBERRY
CRÈME BRULEE TRIFLE

MAKES 1 QUART
The better quality your Vanilla, the better
your Custard

1- Put Sugar into a large heavy skillet and caramelize. Use a heavy duty pot holder to hold the handle of the skillet so you do not burn yourself. Tilt the skillet to evenly brown the sugar or use a wooden spoon. When the Sugar is dark brown, but not burned, immediately turn off the heat and add the Cream. Be very careful because it will bubble up and is very hot. Stirring the bubbling cream and sugar mixture with a wooden spoon will stop the bubbling, but again...be very cautious. Cook until all the Sugar has dissolved.

2- Beat the Egg Yolk with the Half & Half and Vanilla.

3- Place the Egg mixture over a double boiler and begin to heat. Slowly add in the Sugar & Cream mixture. Stir with a wire whisk.

4- Cook your Custard mixture over medium heat for about 20-25 minutes until it will coat a wooden spoon.

5- Pour into another bowl and refrigerate. The Custard should be completely cooled before you make your Trifle.

6- To make a Trifle you simply layer Angel Food Cake, Custard, Fruit and Whipped Cream. You can make in Trifle bowl or in individual servings.

Ingredients for Crème Brulee Custard		
•	2 cups	Sugar
•	1 pint	Heavy Cream
•	8	Egg Yolks
•	1 1/2 cups	Half & Half
•	2 tbls.	Vanilla Extract

Ingredients for Trifle		
•	4 cups	Cubed Angel Food Cake
•	3 cups	Blackberries
•	1 cup	Sugar

Fondue Island Style

Menu

Rum Punch

Corn & Shrimp Fritters

Fondue
Halibut and Shrimp
Yams and Plantains

Sauce Chien

Black Beans Caribe
Saffron Rice

Marinated Cucumbers & Onions

Drunken Pineapple with
Mango Sorbet

Some of the best food I have encountered was on the small Island of Guadeloupe in the lesser Antilles.

Guadeloupe cuisine reflects its many cultures. The local Créole specialties combine the finesse of French cuisine with the spice of African cookery and the exoticism of East Indian and South-east Asian recipes. Much like our Louisiana Créole cuisine theirs is a delicious mélange of French, African and Indian influences. I was so impressed with the preparations of the food, everything so fresh, simple and bursting with flavor. Surprisingly, most of the Chefs I encountered were women. I was very taken with a dish called Accras, a fritter made with Salt Cod. It was not the flavor as much as the lightness and texture. I watched how they made them and was amazed at how little flour went into their fritters. I took their technique to develop one of the most popular appetizers at Regina's at the Regis, ChiChi Beignet and Biscuits & Blues, my Corn and Shrimp Fritters. I have used the same technique for my Crab and Eggplant Fritters.

You can use this formula and create many varieties of a perfect Fritter. Fondue is an ideal dinner for two or four people. Everyone participates in the cooking so you get to sit at the table and enjoy your guests.

CORN AND SHRIMP FRITTERS

MAKES 4 SERVINGS (about 1 dz. Fritters)
In deep skillet - heat fry oil to 375 degrees.

1- In mixing bowl, add Flour, Salt, Cayenne and Baking Powder. Blend with a whisk or fork. Then add the minced Garlic and mix again.

2- "16-21 count Shrimp" mean that there are approximately that many Shrimp to the pound. Your fish supplier will understand that terminology. The Shrimp should be cut into 1/4 inch pieces. You want the Shrimp to be uncooked, peeled, de-veined.

3- Separate Egg Yolk and Egg White. Whip Egg White until stiff but still wet.

4- Mix the Egg Yolk with the Shrimp, Corn Kernels, Green Onions, Fresh Basil. Do not over mix- this will bruise the Corn Kernels and make the batter too wet.

5- Mix the Flour mixture with the Shrimp mixture with a rubber spatula.

6- Fold in the Whipped Egg White.

7- Take two Tablespoons and form 1 inch Fritters and drop into heated Oil. You can stick a wooden skewer in to make sure it is cooked all the way through. If raw batter comes out, let if cook longer.

Ingredients for Corn and Shrimp Fritters

1/2 cups	Flour
1/2 teas.	Salt
1/4 teas.	Cayenne
1 1/2 teas.	Baking Powder
1 1/2 teas.	Minced Garlic
1 cup	Uncooked, Peeled Shrimp (I prefer 16-21 count Shrimp)
1 cup	Fresh Yellow Corn Kernels
1/4 cup	Chopped Green Onions
1 tbls.	Chopped Fresh Basil
1	Egg

Rum Punch

MAKES 8 RUM PUNCHES

- 1/4 CUP OF POWDERED SUGAR DISSOLVED IN 1/4 CUP OF WATER
- 1/2 CUP PINEAPPLE JUICE
- 1/2 CUP ORANGE JUICE
- 1/4 CUP FRESH LIME JUICE
- 6 DASHES OF ANGOSTURA BITTERS
- 1 CUP OF DARK RUM

SERVE OVER CRUSHED ICE

Fondue Island Style
Halibut, Shrimp, Yams & Plantains
with Sauce Chien

MAKES 4 SERVINGS
You will need a fondue pot with fuel and four fondue forks.

This is great for an intimate dinner party of four.
You prepare everything ahead and you cook at the table. It makes for a nice leisurely dinner and you can be at the table throughout the entire dinner.

1- Peel the Yams, slice 1/4 inch thick and cook in boiling water for 8-10 minutes.

2- Peel and slice a ripened Plantain into 1/4 inch slices. *The Plantain is from the Banana family, from the Caribbean, Central and South America. They are often green in the grocery store but like a Banana should not be refrigerated and will ripen on their own with time. You want the Plantain to turn black so it is sweet.*

3- Cut the Halibut into cubes. Season with Salt and Garlic Powder.

4- Season Shrimp with the Goya Sazon con Azafran. It is fairly salty so sprinkle lightly.

5- Arrange on a platter or several plates and refrigerate until needed.

6- Put Oil in fondue pot, filling half full. Preheat on stove to 350 degrees. Keep on stove until ready to use. *You can't get it hot enough using the fuel. This will only keep it hot once you have gotten it to temperature. None of the ingredients take a long cooking time so the heat should hold long enough. If not, take the pot back to the stove for a few minutes if needed.*

7- Cook Halibut, Shrimp, Yams and Plantains in Oil.

Sauce Chien
1- Heat Vinegar in small sauce pan. Add Salt and Sugar.

2- Slice Jalapeno into 1/8 inch rounds leaving seeds attached. Add Peppers to Vinegar.

3- Let set at least three hours.

This is a Dipping Sauce for the cooked Fish and Shrimp.

Ingredients for Fondue Island Style

- 1 lb. Halibut
- 12 Medium Peeled Shrimp
- 2 Medium Yams
- 1 Plantain (ripe)
- 1 qt. Peanut Oil or Vegetable Oil
- 1 pkg. Goya brand Sazon con Azafran

This spice blend is found in the gourmet section of the grocery, usually near Caribbean products. Goya is a widely distributed brand. This will be used to season the Shrimp as well as the Black Beans Caribe. **If you can't find this brand of seasoning mix you can make one: 2 teas. Salt, 1 teas. Garlic Powder, 1/8 teas. Cumin, 1/8 teas. Turmeric and 1/8 teas. Saffron Powder.**

Ingredients for Sauce Chien

- 1 cup White Vinegar
- 1 teas. Salt
- 1 tbls. Sugar
- 1 Red Jalapeno

BLACK BEANS CARIBE

MAKES 4-6 SERVINGS
You will need a heavy 3 qt. pot with a lid.

1- Rinse Black Beans. In heavy pot add Black Beans and cover with water, bring to a boil. Turn off heat and let stand for 1/2 hour. Strain and put the Black Beans back into the pot, add 6 cups of water. Bring Beans back to a boil and then turn down to a simmer.

2- In sauté pan, over medium heat, pour Olive Oil then add Diced Onions, Peppers and Garlic. Sauté until soft. Add to Black Beans.

3- Add Seasoning to Beans and simmer for about an hour. Stir the Beans every 10-15 minutes and check for doneness.

These can be made the day before. This recipe makes a little more than you need for four servings. The cooked Black Beans freeze well and you can use them in soup or on Nachos.

Ingredients for Black Beans Caribe

- 1 lb.   Black Beans
- 2 tbls.   Olive Oil
- 4 cloves   Minced Garlic
- 1/2 cup   Diced Onion
- 1/2 cup   Diced Peppers
- 1 teas.   Goya brand Sazon con Azafran

SAFFRON RICE

Ingredients for Saffron Rice

- 2 cups   Long Grain Rice
- 4 cups   Water
- 1/2 teas.   Salt
- 1/2 teas.   Garlic
- 1/8 teas.   Saffron Threads
  (or 3 grams of Saffron Threads)
- 1 teas.   Orange Rind
- 3 tbls.   Butter

MAKES 4 SERVINGS

1- In heavy 2 qt. pot add Rice, Water, Salt and Garlic.

2- Bring to a boil. Add Saffron Threads and grated Orange Rind. Stir in and lower heat to a low simmer. Cover with a lid. Cook for 15 minutes with the Rice covered.

3- Add Butter and stir Rice grains with a fork. The Rice should be dry and all grains separated. If the Rice is not dry it may need to continue to simmer for another five minutes at a time. Test for doneness. Adjust Salt if needed.

Marinated Cucumbers & Onions

MAKES 4 SERVINGS

1- Peel and slice Cucumber.

2- Peel Red Onion, cut in half then slice into thin strips.

3- Put Cucumbers and Red Onions in small glass bowl and add Salt, Sugar, Lime Juice and Vinegar. Toss well.

4- Let sit for at least one hour before serving.

5- Serve as a condiment with Rice and Beans.

Ingredients for Marinated Cucumbers & Onions		
•	1	Cucumber
•	1	Red Onion
•	1/2 teas.	Salt
•	1 tbls.	Sugar
•	1 tbls.	Fresh Lime Juice
•	1 teas.	Vinegar

Drunken Pineapple over Mango Sorbet

MAKES 4 SERVINGS

1- In large sauté pan, over medium heat, melt Butter, then add Brown Sugar.

2- Add Lime Juice, continue to cook until Brown Sugar has cooked to a syrup.

3- Add fresh Pineapple Cubes to the Brown Sugar syrup in the pan.

4- Add the Rum (be careful it may flame up). Heat for just about 60 seconds so the alcohol will reduce.

5- Spoon warm Pineapple flavored syrup over Mango Sorbet.

6- Garnish with a slice of Star Fruit.

Ingredients for Drunken Pineapple		
•	2 cups	Fresh Pineapple Cubes
•	1/4 lb.	Butter
•	1 cup	Brown Sugar
•	1 teas.	Fresh Lime Juice
•	4 tbls.	Dark Rum
•	1 pt.	Mango Sorbet
•	1	Star Fruit

Mississippi Fish Dinner

Menu

Wedge Salad
with
Blue Cheese and Tomatoes

Fresh Corn Maque Choux

Jalapeno Hushpuppies

Catfish Filets
in White Corn Meal
with Smoked Tomato Coulis &
Blackeye Pea Vinaigrette

Blueberry Custard Tarts

WEDGE SALAD WITH BLUE CHEESE & TOMATOES

MAKES 8 SERVINGS

1- Cut Iceberg Lettuce into quarters. Place on serving platter.

2- Cut Ripe Tomatoes into quarters and arrange with Lettuce, then refrigerate.

3- In small mixing bowl whisk together Red Wine Vinegar, Olive Oil, Sugar and Salt.

4- When ready to serve drizzle Vinegar and Oil mixture over chilled Iceberg Lettuce and Tomatoes.

5- Sprinkle Blue Cheese on top of Lettuce and Tomatoes and serve.

Ingredients for Iceberg Lettuce with Blue Cheese and Tomatoes

• 2	Small Heads of Iceberg Lettuce
• 4	Ripe Red Tomatoes
• 8 oz.	Crumbled Blue Cheese
• 1/4 cup	Red Wine Vinegar
• 1/2 cup	Olive Oil
• 1 teas.	Sugar
• 1/8 teas.	Salt

FRESH CORN MAQUE CHOUX

MAKES 8 SERVINGS

1- Cut Kernels off of Corn. Cut Tomatoes into quarters, using your thumbs push all of the seeds out of the Tomatoes. Dice the Tomatoes, Onions and Peppers the same size as the Corn Kernels.

2- In heavy pot add Butter and Oil, heat to a medium heat.

3- Add Onions and Peppers and cook until soft, about 5-6 minutes.

4- Add Corn Kernels and cook for 5 minutes. Stir frequently so the Corn Kernels cook evenly.

5- Add the Tomatoes and Green Onions and cook for another 5 minutes.

6- Taste and season with Salt and Pepper.

Ingredients for Fresh Corn Maque Choux

• 1/4 lb.	Butter
• 2 teas.	Vegetable Oil
• 1/2 cup	Minced Onion
• 1/2 cup	Minced Sweet Pepper (red or green)
• 6 ears	Fresh Sweet Yellow Corn
• 2	Ripe Tomatoes
• 1/2 cup	Minced Green Onions
•	Salt and White or Cayenne Pepper to taste

This recipe was given to me by my Great Auntie from Opelousas, Louisiana, Marie Trosclair Caldwell. "Nan Marie" and her sister Corrine Trosclair were a great culinary inspirations to my father J.P. Trosclair. Nan Marie was 90 when she gave this recipe to me. When she was giving me the recipe she asked if I liked Sweet Basil. I said yes. She said, "so do I darlin', but not in my Maque Choux". Nan Marie lived just short of her 98th birthday and she had a touch with a wooden spoon all of her days.

Jalapeno Hushpuppies

MAKES 8 SERVINGS

1- In metal or ceramic mixing bowl blend Corn Meal, Flour, Baking Soda and Baking Powder.

2- Add Green Onions to Flour mixture. Stir until evenly distributed.

3- In small bowl beat Egg into Buttermilk until well blended. Add the minced Jalapeno.

4- Add Egg and Buttermilk mixture to Flour mixture, blend with wire whisk.

5- Let stand for 15 minutes. Roll into 1 inch balls.

6- Using an electric fryer or cast iron skillet, heat Peanut Oil to 375 degrees.

7- Using a slotted spoon, gently drop Hushpuppies into hot Oil. Cook until golden brown, about 3-4 minutes.

8- Drain on paper towel to remove excess grease. Serve hot.

Ingredients for Jalapeno Hushpuppies

- 2 cups — Corn Meal
- 1/4 cup — Flour
- 1/2 teas. — Baking Soda
- 1 teas. — Baking Powder
- 1/2 cup — Chopped Green Onions
- 2 teas. — Minced Pickled Jalapeno
- 1 1/4 cup — Buttermilk
- 1 — Egg
- 1 qt. — Peanut Oil

Catfish in White Corn Meal

MAKES 8 SERVINGS

1- The best fried Catfish is thin and crispy. With a sharp boning knife or an electric knife- cut the Catfish Filets in half length-wise so you have thin Filets. Cut each thin Filet into three pieces at an angle. The finished Catfish Filets should be 1/4 thick and 3 or 4 inches long.

2- Lightly Salt and Pepper each Catfish Filet.

3- Beat Eggs with Milk to make Egg Wash for Fish.

4- Mix White Corn Meal, Flour, Salt, Garlic Powder and Cayenne Pepper.

5- Heat Peanut Oil to 375 degrees.

6- Dip each Filet into Egg Wash, then into seasoned Corn Meal mixture. Make sure it is well coated.

7- Fry each Catfish Filet until golden brown. If the Oil is not very deep it is best to turn each Filet over to brown evenly.

Ingredients for Catfish in White Corn Meal

- 4 lbs. — Catfish Filets

Salt and Pepper

- 2 — Eggs
- 2 cups — Milk
- 2 cups — White Corn Meal
- 1/2 cup — Flour
- 1/2 teas. — Salt
- 1/2 teas. — Garlic Powder
- 1/4 teas. — Cayenne Pepper
- 1 qt. — Peanut Oil

I smoke Tomatoes with Olive Oil, Sea Salt and Cracked Black Pepper- I put the tomatoes in a pan and use Hickory Chips and Smoke for about an hour for a deep smoked flavor. But, when weather or time does not permit...I take this short cut. It works quite well for the smoked tomato coulis. My recipe for Smoked Tomatoes is on page 235.

Oven Smoked Tomatoes

1 dozen Roma Tomatoes - cut in quarters

Lay on Baking Sheet (with sides- not a flat sheet)

Mix ½ cup of Olive Oil with 3 tbls. of Liquid Hickory Smoke

Drizzle over cut Roma Tomatoes then sprinkle with

1 tbls. Sea Salt

1 tbls. Cracked Black Pepper

Bake at 300 degrees for 45 Minutes

To Make Smoked Tomato Coulis

MAKES 2 qts. of Smoked Tomato Coulis
(this freezes well and is great to have on hand)
1- Place large pot over medium heat, add Olive Oil.
2- Cut Onion into 8 pieces and Carrots into 4 pieces and sauté for 5 minutes.
3- In same pot add Tomatoes, Jalapenos, Basil, Garlic and Bay Leaves. Cook over medium heat for 35-40 minutes.
4- Remove Bay Leaves and pour into food processor.
5- Use the pulse button of the processor. This sauce should be a coarse puree- not soupy.

Variations and other uses for Tomato Coulis-
This makes a wonderful Base for Cream of Tomato Soup. Just add one part Chicken Stock, one part Tomato Coulis and one part Cream.
You can add one part Cream, one part Tomato Coulis and use as a Pasta Sauce.
The Smoked Tomato Coulis is an excellent base for a Gazpacho. Add diced Cucumber, Red Onion and Tomato Juice to get the proper consistency.

Ingredients for Oven Smoked Tomatoes

- 1 dz. Roma Tomatoes
- 1/2 cup Olive Oil
- 3 tbls. Liquid Hickory Smoke
- 1 tbls. Sea Salt
- 1 tbls. Cracked Black Pepper

Ingredients for Smoked Tomato Coulis

- 2 tbls. Olive Oil
- 1 medium Onion
- 3 medium Carrots
- 3 cups Canned, Diced Tomatoes in juice
- 1 dozen Smoked Roma Tomatoes
- 2 tbls. Pickled Jalapeno
- 8 each Fresh Basil Leaves
- 5 cloves Garlic
- 2 each Bay Leaves

Blackeye Pea Vinaigrette

MAKES 8 SERVINGS

1- Rinse Blackeye Peas, so they are not "starchy" and chill.

2- In blender or food processor puree Shallots.

3- Add Cider Vinegar, Brown Sugar, Salt and blend.

4- Slowly add Oil to emulsify. Pour into a bowl.

5- Then add Blackeye Peas, Julienne of Green Onions and toss in Vinaigrette.

6- Chill and use to top hot Catfish right before serving.

To assemble dish:
1- Place warmed Smoked Tomato Coulis on Plate.

2- Top with hot Catfish in White Corn Meal Crust.

3- Spoon over warm Black Eye Pea Vinaigrette.
This can be served on individual plates or on a platter family style.

Serve Immediately.

Ingredients for Blackeye Pea Vinaigrette

- 2 each — Shallots
- 1/3 cup — Cider Vinegar
- 2/3 cup — Light Salad Oil
- 2 teas. — Brown Sugar
- 1 teas. — Salt
- 1/2 cup — Julienne Green Onion
- 2 cups — Cooked Blackeye Peas

102

JALAPENO TARTAR SAUCE

MAKES 8 SERVINGS
This will keep in the refrigerator for five or six days. If you use homemade mayonnaise keep for just two days.

1- In food processor add Jalapenos, Capers, Pickles, Green Onion and Cilantro. Pulse until the ingredients are minced evenly.

2- In glass bowl blend Mayonnaise and Sour Cream, then add minced Jalapeno mixture.

3- Add the Lime Juice and grated Lime Peel. Stir well and keep chilled.

Ingredients for Jalapeno Tartar Sauce

•	3 tbls.	Pickled Jalapenos
•	1 tbls.	Capers
•	1/4 cup	Dill Pickles
•	1/4 cup	Green Onion
•	2 tbls.	Cilantro
•	1 cup	Mayonnaise
•	1/4 cup	Sour Cream
•	1 tbls.	Fresh Lime Juice
•	1 teas.	Grated Lime Peel

Ingredients for Blueberry Custard Tarts

•	12 each	3 inch unbaked Tart Shells
•	6	Egg Yolks
•	3/4 cup	Sugar
•	2 cups	Heavy Whipping Cream
•	1 pint	Blueberries

BLUEBERRY CUSTARD TARTS

MAKES 8 SERVINGS

1- Place 3 inch unbaked Tart Shells on baking sheet with space between, so they can brown evenly.

2- Evenly distribute the Blueberries into each of the unbaked Tart Shells.

3- In mixing bowl using a wooden spoon mix Egg Yolks and Sugar into a smooth paste. The Egg Yolks should be blended with the Sugar but you should not whip and create air bubbles for a Custard.

4- Stir in the Heavy Cream and then pour into unbaked Tart Shells.

5- Bake at 350 degrees for 40 minutes.

I PREFER DUTCH ANN TART SHELLS (THEY HAPPEN TO BE MADE IN NATCHEZ). IF YOU CANNOT FIND INDIVIDUAL TART SHELLS IN THE FROZEN SECTION OF YOUR GROCERY, YOU CAN BUY PRE MADE PIE CRUST AND MAKE YOUR OWN QUITE QUICKLY.

YOU MAY SUBSTITUTE BLACKBERRIES OR RASPBERRIES IF YOU LIKE.

Summer Grill
Menu

Roasted Pepper & Olive
Salad
with Grilled Bread

Green Tomato & Shrimp
Skewers

Rib Eye & Potato
Skewers

Grilled Corn on the Cob
With
Chili Lime Butter

Key Lime
Frozen Soufflé

Roasted Pepper & Olive Salad

MAKES 8 SERVINGS

1- Preheat oven to 400 degrees. Spray baking sheet with Oil. Place Red Bell Peppers on baking sheet.

2- Put Peppers in oven and roast for 20 minutes.

3- Quarter Roma Tomatoes, Salt and Pepper the Roma Tomato quarters and place on baking sheet with Red Peppers and roast for another 12-15 minutes.

4- Peel skin off roasted Red Peppers. Cut in half and remove the seeds. Then slice Peppers into 1/2 inch strips.

5- Arrange mixed Salad Greens on platter, then arrange roasted Roma Tomatoes around the edges. Put roasted Red Peppers down the center. Arrange the Kalmata Olives around the Peppers.

6- In small bowl mix Vinegar, Olive Oil, Salt and Sugar. Drizzle over Salad and serve.

Ingredients for Roasted Pepper and Olive Salad

- 4   Red Bell Peppers
- 8   Roma Tomatoes
- 4 cups   Mixed Salad Greens
- 1/4 cup   Kalmata Olives
- 1/4 cup   Balsamic Vinegar
- 1/4 teas.   Salt
- 1 teas.   Sugar
- 1/2 cup   Olive Oil

Grilled Bread

MAKES 8 SERVINGS

1- In small bowl mix Olive Oil, Garlic, Parsley and Salt.

2- Using pastry brush, brush both sides of sliced Country Style French or Italian Bread.

3- After you have grilled all of your main items, clean the grill. Brush the grill with Oil (be careful, as the Oil will flame if you use too much).

4- Grill the Bread for just a minute. Then turn and grill the other side. Serve immediately.

Ingredients for Grilled Bread

- 16 slices   Country Style French or Italian Bread
- 1/4 cup   Olive Oil
- 2 tbls.   Minced Garlic
- 1 tbls.   Minced Parsley
- 1/4 teas.   Kosher Salt

Green Tomato & Shrimp Skewers

MAKES 8 SERVINGS

You will need 16 (8 for Shrimp and 8 for Beef) eight inch wooden skewers or metal skewers. If you use wooden- soak them beforehand in water for one hour so they don't burn on the grill.

1- Cut Green Tomatoes into quarters.

2- Skewer Shrimp, Tomato, Shrimp. Each Skewer should have three Shrimp and two Tomato quarters.

3- In small sauce pan add Orange Marmalade, Vinegar, Brown Sugar, Green Peppercorns and Salt. Cook over medium heat until all Sugar is dissolved.

4- Salt and Pepper Shrimp skewers and grill. When half cooked, brush on Glaze. Pour extra Glaze over Skewered Shrimp & Green Tomatoes before serving.

Ingredients for Green Tomato and Shrimp Skewers		
•	4	Green Tomatoes
•	24	Jumbo Gulf Shrimp

Ingredients for Green Peppercorn Orange Glaze		
•	1/2 cup	Orange Marmalade
•	3 tbls.	Cider Vinegar
•	1 tbls.	Brown Sugar
•	2 tbls.	Green Peppercorns
•	1/2 teas.	Salt

Rib Eye & Potato Skewers

Ingredients for Rib Eye and Potato Skewers		
•	4	12 oz. Rib Eye of Beef
•	24	Small New Red Potatoes
•	2 tbls.	Minced Garlic
•	1 tbls.	Cracked Black Pepper
•	1 tbls.	Kosher Salt
•	1/4 cup	Olive Oil
•	3 tbls.	Lea & Perrins
•	1 teas.	Fresh Thyme
•	1 teas.	Fresh Rosemary

MAKES 8 SERVINGS

1- Boil New Red Potatoes until tender but not falling apart. A fork should go through with little effort.

2- Cut each 12 oz. Rib Eye into 4 cubes.

3- Skewer Potato, Rib Eye cube, Potato. Each skewer should have three Potatoes and two pieces of Rib Eye.

4- In small bowl mix Garlic, Salt, Pepper, Olive Oil, Lea & Perrins, Thyme and Rosemary.

5- Marinate Rib Eye skewers for at least an hour before grilling.

GRILLED CORN WITH CHILI LIME BUTTER

MAKES 8 SERVINGS

1- Shuck Corn, but leave some of the outer husk attached. Remove all the corn silk.

2- In large pot bring water to a boil. Cook Corn for 5 minutes. Drain all excess water and pat dry.

3- Mix Olive Oil, Salt and Garlic. Brush on Corn and place Corn on grill. Grill and turn Corn to get even grill marks on Corn.

4- Soften Butter, then stir in Lime Peel, Ancho-Chili Powder and Salt.

5- Spread Chili Lime Butter on grilled Corn or serve on the side.

Ingredients for Grilled Corn

- 8 ears — Fresh Corn
- 4 tbls. — Olive Oil
- 1/2 teas. — Salt
- 1 teas. — Garlic

Ingredients for Chili Lime Butter

- 1/4 lb. — Butter
- 1 teas. — Grated Lime Peel
- 1/8 teas. — Ancho-Chili Powder
- 1/8 teas. — Salt

KEY LIME FROZEN SOUFFLÉ

MAKES 8 SERVINGS

1- In heavy sauce pan add 2 cups of Sugar and 1/2 cup Water. Cook until soft ball stage, 115 degrees on a candy thermometer. Let cool.

2- Whip Egg Whites until soft peak stage, then slowly add Sugar Syrup and whip until stiff but not dry.

3- In separate bowl beat Egg Yolks with 2 tbls. of Sugar until ribbon stage or pale yellow. Add Lime Juice and Lime Zest.

4- Whip Cream and fold in Lime mixture.

5- Fold in Egg Whites. Pour Key Lime Soufflé mixture into individual Styrofoam cups. Freeze at least 4 hours before serving.

These can be made days in advance. The Styrofoam cups make them easy to unmold.

Ingredients for Key Lime Soufflé

- 2 cups — Sugar
- 1/2 cup — Water
- 4 — Egg Whites
- 4 — Egg Yolks
- 2 tbls. — Sugar
- 1/2 cup — Key Lime Juice
- 2 tbls. — Lime Zest
- 1 cup — Heavy Cream
- 8 — 8 oz. Styrofoam cups

If you can not find Key Limes, use 3 Limes with 1 Lemon to make your Juice.

A Twin Oaks Summer Wedding

Menu

Twin Oaks Almond Iced Tea
Peach Champagne Cocktails
Watermelon Martinis

Butter Biscuits with Smoked Turkey
and Cranberry Chutney

Tomato Sandwiches with Smoked Bacon

Peppered Brisket of Beef with
Assorted Artisan Breads and Horseradish Sauce

Fried Chicken Wings with Butter Biscuits
and Fig and Kumquat Preserves

Watermelon-Tomato Salad with Mint Vinaigrette

Cast Iron Vegetable Platter

Creamed Spinach & Artichoke with Crabmeat
in Pastry Shells

Smoked Catfish Torta

Black Pepper Torta topped with Caviar

Hot Pepper Jelly Torta
Assorted Crackers

PEACH CHAMPAGNE COCKTAIL

SERVES 12

In small glass pitcher mix

3 oz.   Peach Schnapps
24 oz. Peach Nectar

Divide equally in 12 Fluted Champagne glasses.

Champagne of Choice- I recommend a lower priced Champagne, good Champagne should never be enhanced.

Drop a Mint Leave and Peach slice into each glass, then top with Champagne.

WATERMELON MARTINI

SERVES 12
When preparing the Watermelon Salad on page 117, reserve the Watermelon Juice and a few of the Watermelon Balls for your Watermelon Martinis.

24   Watermelon Balls

Place two Watermelon Balls on a Decorative pick and place in chilled martini glasses.

6 oz.   Watermelon Liquor

12 oz. Fresh Watermelon Juice

12 oz. Skyy Vodka

Fill Martini Shaker with Ice, pour enough for two Martinis at a time into shaker and shake until ice cold, then strain into Martini Glass.

TWIN OAKS
ALMOND ICED TEA

SERVES 25 THIS MAKES TWO PUNCH BOWLS

1- In Gallon Container add Water with 8 Pitcher size Lipton Cold Brew Tea Bags. Brew for 30 minutes.

2- Make a Simple Syrup with 3 cups of Sugar and 1 cup of water. Cook until Sugar has dissolved.

3- Add Simple Syrup and Almond Extract to Concentrated Tea.

4- Fill a punch bowl half way with crushed ice, then pour Almond Ice Tea over.

5- Serve immediately.

Ingredients for Almond Iced Tea		
•	8 each	Pitcher Size Lipton Cold Brew Tea Bags
•	1 gallon	Water
•	3 cups	Sugar
•	1 cup	Water
•	2 oz.	Almond Extract

Almond Iced Tea under the Oak Trees with the Gospel Choir welcoming guests made this wedding one of the most memorable.

BUTTER BISCUITS WITH SMOKED TURKEY AND CRANBERRY CHUTNEY

MAKES 2 DOZEN

1- Bake Biscuits in muffin tins to help shape them evenly.

2- Cut Biscuits in half and fill with sliced Turkey.

3- Spread 1 teaspoon of Cranberry Chutney on top of the Smoked Turkey and place top back on Biscuit.

Ingredients for Butter Biscuits with Smoked Turkey and Cranberry Chutney

- 2 dz.   2 inch Biscuits
            Recipe on page 154
- 2 lbs.   Sliced Smoked Turkey
- 2 cups   Cranberry Chutney
            Recipe on page 172

Ingredients for Horseradish Sauce

- 1 cup   Sour Cream
- 1 cup   Mayonnaise
- 2 teas.   Dijon Mustard
- 1/4 cup   Prepared Horseradish

Optional

- 2 tbls.   Capers

HORSERADISH SAUCE

1- In mixing bowl, blend Sour Cream, Mayonnaise, Dijon Mustard and Horseradish with a wire whisk until smooth.

Serve Chilled
Capers are optional but a nice addition.

TOMATO SANDWICHES WITH SMOKED BACON
RECIPE ON PAGE 65

ROASTED ASPARAGUS
RECIPE ON PAGE 173

BLACK PEPPER MARINADE

Ingredients for Black Pepper Marinade

- 4 tbls.   Chopped Garlic
- 4 tbls.   Chopped Basil
- 4 tbls.   Cracked Black Pepper
- 1/4 lb.   Butter
- 1/4 cup   Olive Oil
- 1/2 cup   Worcestershire Sauce

MAKES 2 CUPS

1- In sauce pan warm Butter, Olive Oil and Worcestershire Sauce.

2- Add Chopped Garlic, Basil and Cracked Black Pepper.

3- Simmer for 15 minutes.

4- Let Marinade stay at room temperature.

Ingredients for Beef Brisket

- 12 lb.   Beef Brisket
- 3 tbls.   Sea Salt
- 1 tbls.   Cracked Black Pepper

PEPPERED BRISKET OF BEEF

WHEN SLICING BRISKET, first you trim away any excess fat, then you slice against the grain.

*ARTISAN BREADS....
I am always looking for good breads. I love the breads from LaBrea Bakery in Los Angeles. They are sold all over the country. For those of you who live in a city with good bakeries...you are very lucky. Because there is no bakery in Natchez I often buy breads from Whole Foods or other gourmet stores and keep them in my freezer. Good bread makes all the difference.*

MAKES 12 SERVINGS

This dish is best made a day or two ahead.
1- Preheat oven to 425 degrees.

2- Season Brisket with Sea Salt and Pepper.

3- Place fat side up in heavy roasting pan uncovered.

4- Cook in 425 degree oven for 40 minutes until the fat of the Brisket is browned.

5- Reduce the temperature to 375 degrees.

6- Add the Marinade and 2 cups of Water, cover with foil and place back in oven for 2 hours more.

7- Remove from oven and pour drippings into a pan. Let drippings cool so fat congeals and can be removed.

8- Remove Fat (if you like to use everything...like I do, keep in zip lock bags in the freezer and use in Bread and Cornbread Dressings it adds a richness that can not be duplicated). Save the drippings to pour over the sliced Brisket.

9- Slice Brisket, pour drippings over sliced meat, heat and serve.

Fried chicken wings

Heat Fry Oil to 360-370 degrees

1- Rinse Drumettes then place in large metal bowl. Cover with Water approx. 2 qts. Add 1/2 cup of Franks Hot Sauce or Crystal Hot Sauce, then add Salt, Garlic Powder and Pepper. Place in refrigerator for at least two hours or as long as overnight.

2- Mix Salt and Pepper into Flour. Roll about four Chicken Drumettes at a time through flour. Coat well and drop into hot Oil. Fry until they float to the top, approx. 10-12 minutes.

Serve with Tiny Biscuits (recipe on page 154) and Fig and Kumquat Preserves

Ingredients for Fried Chicken Wings

- 3 dz.   Chicken Drumettes
- 1/2 cup Hot Sauce
- 1 tbls.   Salt
- 1 tbls.   Garlic Powder
- 1 tbls.   Black Pepper
- 2 qts.   Water
- 3 cups   Flour
- 1 teas.   Salt
- 2 teas.   Black Pepper

Fry Oil for Fryer or Electric Skillet

Fig & Kumquat Preserves

Ingredients for Fig & Kumquat Preserves

- 1 lb.   Figs with skin on
- 8 oz.   Kumquats
- 2 lbs.   Sugar

This recipe is not large enough to go to the trouble to can in Jelly Jars. I just freeze in plastic freezer containers. My ratio is equal Sugar to Fruit. If you have 5 lbs. of Fruit then add 5 lbs. of Sugar.

1- Wash and dry Kumquats. Slice into very thin rounds. Using the tip of your paring knife, remove any large seeds.

2- In heavy saucepan add Kumquats and Sugar. Slowly cook until Sugar is dissolved. Cook over medium heat for half an hour before adding the Figs.

3- Wash and dry Figs. I like using the whole Fig leaving the skin and stem on. It makes a better preserve and looks nicer with whole Figs in the Preserves.

4- Add the Figs and continue to cook for 90 more minutes on low heat. This should produce an amber colored, very rich preserve. If it is getting to that point before the 90 minutes, turn off the heat and transfer into a metal bowl to cool.

Watermelon Tomato Salad
With Mint Vinaigrette

SERVES 12

1- Cut Watermelon in half, remove visible row of black seeds. Using melon baller, scoop small Watermelon Balls. Make the same size as the small Grape Tomatoes. If you can only find Cherry Tomatoes cut them in half. Make the Melon Balls the same size and cut in half as well.

2- Drain the Melon Balls and save the Watermelon juice for cocktails. This can be frozen and used later.

3- Toss the Watermelon and Tomatoes with Mint Vinaigrette and chill for at least one hour.

4- When ready to serve lightly dress Baby Greens with Mint Vinaigrette and top with Watermelon Salad.

5- Julienne Fresh Mint and sprinkle on top of Salad.

Ingredients for Watermelon Salad		
• 1 lb.	Mixed Baby Greens	
• 1 pint	Watermelon Balls	
• 2 pints	Ripe Grape Tomatoes	

Fresh Mint for Garnish

Optional-

You can sprinkle Feta Cheese on top of this and it is a delicious Summer Salad.

Ingredients for Mint Vinaigrette		
• 1/2 cup	Seasoned Rice Vinegar	
• 1 tbls.	Sugar	
• 1 teas.	Salt	
• 1/4 cup	Salad Oil	
• 1 dozen	Julienne Fresh Mint Leaves	

Mint Vinaigrette

1- In glass or metal mixing bowl dissolve Sugar and Salt in the Seasoned Rice Vinegar.

2- Whisk in Salad Oil.

3- Add Julienne of Fresh Mint

Let Vinaigrette sit for 1 hour at room temperature before using.

CREAMED SPINACH & ARTICHOKE WITH CRAB MEAT IN PASTRY SHELLS

MAKES 36 HORS D'OEUVRES

1- In large sauce pan pour a cup of Water with one teaspoon of Salt and bring to a boil. Add Fresh Spinach and push down into pot until Spinach is wilted and bright green. Pour into a colander and let all excess water drain. Chop evenly, do not puree in food processor. You should chop with a knife.

2- In sauté pan add two 2 tbls. Butter and add Minced Onion and cook until soft, about 5 minutes, add Garlic and Heavy Cream, then add Cream Cheese, that has been cut into 8 cubes, one a time until it is melted into the sauce.

3- Drain Marinated Artichoke Hearts and coarsely chop. Add to Mixture.

4- Mix Spinach in and stir until all ingredients are evenly blended and warm.

5- Add the Lump Crab meat and do not over mix.

6- Pour Mixture into a round Chafing Dish and serve with one inch Tart Shells or Phyllo Cups.

Ingredients for Creamed Spinach with Artichoke and Crab Meat

•	1 lb.	Fresh Spinach with stems Removed
•	3 tbls.	Butter
•	1/4 cup	Minced Onion
•	2 teas.	Minced Garlic
•	8 oz.	Cream Cheese
•	4 oz.	Heavy Cream
•	1 cup	Marinated Artichoke Hearts
•	1 lbs.	Lump Crab Meat
•	3 dozen	small Tart Shells or Phyllo Cups

BLACK PEPPER TORTA TOPPED WITH CAVIAR

MAKES 9 INCH TORTA WHICH SERVES 30

You will need a 9 inch Spring Form Pan, spray well with Spray Oil
1- In large metal bowl add Cream Cheese that has been cut into 1 oz. cubes and Butter that has been cut into 1 oz. cubes and allow to get to room temperature.

2- Once Cream Cheese and Butter has softened, using an Electric Mixer whip the two together, slowly blending in the Sour Cream. This should be blended smoothly with no lumps.

3- Add Garlic Powder, Dill and Grated Lemon Rind. Blend until evenly distributed.

4- Spray spring form pan generously with spray oil such as Pam. Coat the pan with the Cracked Black Pepper, lining the bottom and side of the pan.

5- Pour the Cream Cheese Mixture into the pan and refrigerate over night.

6- Loosen the sides and tap gently to unmold. I turn it over on a decorative cake plate and then top with Caviar. Serve with Crackers or Toast points.

Ingredients for Black Pepper Torta with Caviar

•	32 oz.	Cream Cheese
•	1/2 lb.	Butter
•	1 cup	Sour Cream
•	1 tbls.	Garlic Powder
•	1 teas.	Dill
•	2 teas.	Grated Lemon Rind
•	4 tbls.	Cracked Black Pepper
•	4 oz.	Red Tobikko "Flying Fish Roe" or any reasonably priced Caviar

SMOKED CATFISH TORTA

MAKES 9 INCH TORTA WHICH SERVES 30

You will need a 9 inch Spring Form Pan, spray well with Spray Oil

1- In large metal bowl add Cream Cheese that has been cut into 1 oz. cubes and Butter that has been cut into 1 oz. cubes and allow to get to room temperature.

2- Once Cream Cheese and Butter has softened, using an electric mixer whip the two together, slowly blending in the Sour Cream. This should be blended smoothly with no lumps. Add Garlic Powder and Cajun Spice. Blend until evenly distributed.

3- Chop Hard Boiled Eggs and mix with 1 tbls. Mayonnaise. Use this to line the bottom of the Pan.

4- Take a third of the mixture and spread evenly on top of the Egg Crust.

5-Take 1/2 pound of the Smoked Catfish and chop into small pieces and put on top of this layer of the Cream Cheese mixture.

6- Take another third of the mixture and spread evenly on top of the Catfish.

Ingredients for Smoked Catfish Torta		
•	32 oz.	Cream Cheese
•	1/2 lb.	Butter
•	1 cup	Sour Cream
•	1 teas	Garlic Powder
•	1 teas.	Cajun Spice
Ingredients for Layers		
•	6	Hard Boiled Eggs
•	1 tbls.	Mayonnaise
•	1/2 cup	Minced Red Onion
•	1/4 cup	Capers
•	1 lb.	Smoked Catfish

7- Sprinkle the minced Red Onion and Capers on top of this layer. Then add the last of the Cream Cheese Mixture. Cover with plastic wrap and refrigerate over night.

8- Loosen the sides and tap gently to unmold. Turn it over on a decorative plate and then top with the left over 8 oz. of Smoked Catfish. Slice into thin strips and place in a circular design on top. Serve with Crackers or Toast points.

HOT PEPPER JELLY TORTA

MAKES 9 INCH TORTA WHICH SERVES 30

You will need a 9 inch Spring Form Pan, spray well with Spray Oil

1- In large metal bowl add Cream Cheese that has been cut into 1 oz. cubes and Butter that has been cut into 1 oz. cubes and allow to get to room temperature.

2- Once Cream Cheese and Butter has softened, using an electric mixer whip the two together, slowly blending in the Sour Cream. This should be blended smoothly with no lumps.

3- Place half the Cream cheese mixture into the spring form pan. Then starting from the center of the Torta, add 1 cup of Hot Pepper Jelly. Make sure it is not too close to the edge. If it seems to be, use less Jelly.

4- Add the rest of the Cream Cheese mixture. Cover and refrigerate over night.
Loosen the sides and tap gently to unmold. Turn it over on a decorative plate and then top with the rest of the Pepper Jelly.
I often use Seasoned Pecans and Rosemary on the side for decoration.

Ingredients for Hot Pepper Jelly Torta		
•	32 oz.	Cream Cheese
•	1/2 lb.	Butter
•	1 cup	Sour Cream
•	2 cups	Green or Red Hot Pepper Jelly

Serve with Crackers.

Fall at Twin Oaks
The heart of sharing

Fall at Twin Oaks is my personal favorite time of year

and it brings out some of my favorite recipes—Stuffed French Toast, Pumpkin Chili, Smoked Tomato and Lobster Bisque with Sweet Corn, Gumbo, Braised Beef Ribs and my Thanksgiving Dinner which just about covers the entire food chain. I love Thanksgiving because it is so much more about food, family and friends.

When I moved into Twin Oaks I decided to take on the Sanguinetti family Thanksgiving. I am seventh generation Natchezian and my Mothers sixth generation had hosted Holidays for over 60 years and it only seemed right. Even though the guest list is in the one hundred twenty five range, Thanksgiving is the Holiday I choose to do all the cooking (except for the Smoked Turkey, that I delegate to my brother Peter who owns the Natchez Biscuits and Blues). I would venture to say that the most volume of food cooked in my Kitchen is during the fall. Thanksgiving has a lot to do with that, the fact that I have five sisters, three brothers and then you add in brothers and sister in laws, fourteen nieces and nephews, forty two first cousins and I have no idea how many spouses and children they have total. All of those are directly related on my Mothers side of the family. So, now you understand why I easily have over a hundred for Thanksgiving.

The weather is still warm enough to spend time out side but the changing colors give promise of crisp fall evenings that beg for a menu of Soup for Supper with Crusty Bread and Hot Buttered Rum. October is the month for my Balloon Race lunch with Pumpkin Chili and Candied Apples. Gumbo is perfect for my Thursday night Poker group during the fall months. In this section I also share my recipe for Duck with Fig and Lemon Preserves, one of the most popular dishes at my San Francisco restaurant "Regina's at the Regis". To me it even tastes even better here at Twin Oaks in Natchez.

Stuffed French Toast Breakfast

Menu

Café Mocha

Stuffed French Toast
with
Cinnamon & Orange
Spiced Cream Cheese

Apple Cured Bacon
with
Black Pepper

Apricots in Brandy

CAFÉ MOCHA

MAKES 6 CUPS

1- Brew a pot of strong French Roast Coffee.

2- In small sauce pan mix Half & Half and Ghirardelli Sweet Ground Chocolate, warm over medium heat, remove when steam begins to form.

3- Whip Cream to stiff peaks, place in pastry bag with a star tip for a nice presentation or you may just spoon on top (it's ok to buy canned Whipped Cream if you are pressed for time).

4- In decorative coffee cups, pour 1/4 cup (approx. 2 oz.) of Chocolate mixture then pour about 4 oz. of strong Coffee, top with Whipped Cream and a Chocolate Covered Coffee Bean. Add a stick of Cinnamon or you can sprinkle Cinnamon Sugar on top if you like a sweeter drink.

Ingredients for Café Mocha

- 4 tbls.   Ground French Roast Coffee (makes 4 cups of Coffee for recipe)
- 6 tbls.   Ghirardelli Sweet Ground Chocolate
- 1 1/2 cups   Half & Half
- 1 cup   Whipping Cream
- 6   Cinnamon Sticks or Cinnamon Sugar
- 6   Chocolate Covered Coffee Beans

STUFFED FRENCH TOAST

MAKES 6 SLICES

1- To make Stuffing, in food processor add softened Cream Cheese, Powdered Sugar, 1/4 teas. Cinnamon, 2 teas. Grated Orange Peel, blend until smooth.

2- Take six slices of Cinnamon Bread and spread 1 heaping tablespoon of Stuffing on each slice, top with other six slices.

3- Prepare Batter in medium mixing bowl, add Eggs and beat well, add Half and Half, 1/4 teas. Cinnamon and 1 teas. Grated Orange Peel.

4- Dip each stuffed Cinnamon Bread in Batter.

5- In nonstick pan add 1 tbls. Butter. Brown French Toast on each side then place on a baking sheet. Repeat until you have all six done.

6- Place into 350 degree oven for 8-10 minutes before serving.

Ingredients for Stuffed French Toast

- 12 slices   Cinnamon Bread
- 1/2 teas.   Cinnamon
- 3 teas.   Grated Orange Peel
- 3 tbls.   Powdered Sugar
- 8 oz.   Cream Cheese
- 1 cup   Half & Half
- 3 each   Eggs
- 6 tbls.   Butter

APRICOTS IN BRANDY

MAKES 3 CUPS

1- Soak Dried Apricots in Brandy for several hours (preferably the night before).

2- In small sauce pan, melt Butter over medium heat, add Brown Sugar and dissolve. Add Brandy soaked Apricots, turn heat down and cook for another ten minutes until Syrup has thickened.

Ingredients for Apricots in Brandy

- 8 oz.   Dried Apricots
- 2 oz.   Brandy
- 4 tbls.   Butter
- 1 cup   Brown Sugar

Optional Items

- 1/2 cup   Pecans (chopped)
- 1/4 cup   Golden Raisins

Dried Cherries may be substituted for Apricots

APPLE CURED BACON WITH BLACK PEPPER

Ingredients for Bacon with Black Pepper

- 12 thick slices   Apple Cured Bacon
- 1 tbls.   Cracked Black Pepper

MAKES 4 SERVINGS

1- Press Cracked Black Pepper into sliced Bacon. Cook slowly in skillet until Bacon is crisp, about 12-15 minutes.

Take the time to ask your butcher ahead about Apple Cured Bacon. If they don't carry it, they can often get it for you. There are several brands out there. You do want it sliced thick.
The best way to do your Cracked Black Pepper is to begin with whole Peppercorns and grind it in a coffee grinder to get a course grind.

Soup for Supper

Menu

Fall Relish Tray

Crusty Bread Bowls

Smoked Tomato
Wild Rice Chowder
With Sweet Corn & Lobster

Creole Vegetable Soup

Oyster Rockefeller Soup

Three Layer Apple Pie
with Pecan Crust

FALL RELISH TRAY

MAKES 12 SERVINGS

1- Wash and peel Carrots.

2- On baking sheet place Beets, Carrots and Red Peppers. Leave a little space in between.

3- Drizzle with 4 tbls. of Olive Oil and sprinkle with Salt and Pepper.

4- In 400 degree oven roast Vegetables. Carrots will be done first, about 20-25 minutes. A fork should go through the Carrot with ease. Then Red Peppers at about 35 minutes. Skin should be blistered. Then Beets at about 45-60 minutes depending on the size. Once again a fork should go through the Beet with ease to make sure it is done.

5- Cut Carrots in half and then into quarters.

6- Peel whole Red Peppers. Cut off the top and stuff with Boursin Cheese.

7- Peel Beets, cut in half then into quarters. Drizzle with the last 2 tbls. of Olive Oil and 2 tbls. of Balsamic Vinegar. Sprinkle with Salt and Pepper.

8- Arrange on a round tray. Carrot Sticks, Beets, Stuffed Peppers and Olives. Garnish with Toasted French Bread Rounds.

You may substitute any Fall Vegetables you like.
Cheese may be added to this tray or any pickled Vegetables or interesting Olives.

Ingredients for Fall Relish Tray

•	4	Beets
•	4	Carrots
•	2	Red Peppers
•	6 tbls.	Olive Oil
•	2 tbls.	Balsamic Vinegar
•		Salt and Pepper
•	8 oz.	Boursin Cheese
•	1/2 Cup	Jalapeno Olives
•	2 dozen	Toasted French Bread Rounds

Ingredients for Crusty Bread Bowls

•	12	7 to 8 inch French Bread Rounds

CRUSTY BREAD BOWLS

MAKES 12 SERVINGS
These will actually be used as bowls so the key is to get them very crisp so they will hold up to the Soup.
The Bread is wonderful to eat with the flavor of the Soup on it.

Preheat oven to 250 degrees.

1- Cut the top off of each French Bread Round Loaf.

2- Hollow out the center with your hands. Pull all the soft bread out of the center but leave the outside intact.

3- Bake at 250 degrees for about 18-25 minutes. The Bread Bowl should be dry and crisp.

You may do these ahead of time but they should be served warm.

SMOKED TOMATO WILD RICE CHOWDER WITH SWEET CORN AND LOBSTER

MAKES 8 SERVINGS

1- 1 qt. of Shell Fish Stock made from Lobster, Shrimp or Crab Shells. *I don't fret over fish stock, it is easy and just for added flavor. I throw all the ingredients into a stock pot and simmer for 45 minutes then strain.*

2- Use 1/2 cup of Wild Rice to 1 1/2 cups of Water. Cook in heavy sauce pan. Bring to a boil then simmer until grains are soft but not mushy. This takes approx. 35 minutes.

3- Take two cups of fresh Corn Kernels and place in a very hot cast iron skillet to roast.

4- In 6 qt. soup pot add 1 qt. of Smoked Tomato Coulis, Shell Fish Stock, Wild Rice, Corn and 1 qt. of Cream. Simmer for 15 minutes over medium heat.

5- Add the Lobster Meat and simmer for another 5-10 minutes before serving.

Ingredients for Smoked Tomato Wild Rice Chowder		
•	1 qt.	Smoked Tomato Coulis (recipe on page 101)
•	1 qt.	Shell Fish Stock *made with 1 qt. of Water and 4 Gumbo Crabs or shells of 2 Lobsters, 2 teas. Salt and 1 teas. Peppercorns and half of a White Onion. Simmer for 45 minutes and strain.*
•	2 cups	Cooked Wild Rice
•	2 cups	Sweet Corn
•	1 qt.	Cream
•	2 cups	Chopped Lobster Meat

Ingredients for Creole Vegetable Soup		
•	1/2 lb.	Diced Andouille Sausage
•	1	Chopped Onion
•	1	Julienne Bulb of Fennel
•	4	Sliced Cloves of Garlic
•	2	Medium Yams
•	2	Medium Turnips
•	4	Small Red Potatoes
•	2 cups	Mustard Greens
•	1	12 oz. can of Diced Tomatoes in Juice
•	2 qts.	Chicken Stock
•		Salt and Pepper

CREOLE VEGETABLE SOUP

MAKES 8 SERVINGS
The Fennel and Turnips give this Soup wonderful flavor.

1- Peel and dice Yams and Turnips into 3/4 inch cubes. Wash Red Potatoes. Leaving the skin on dice into 3/4 inch cubes.

2- In heavy soup pot heat diced Andouille, add Chopped Onion, Julienne of Fennel then cook until Onions begin to caramelize and begin to brown.

3- Add Garlic, Yams, Turnips and Potatoes.

4- Add canned Diced Tomatoes with the Juice and add the Chicken Stock or Water. Let cook for 30 minutes.

5- Cut the cleaned Mustard Greens into 1 inch pieces then add to the Soup and let simmer for another 20 minutes. Adjust Salt and Pepper.

Oyster Rockefeller Soup

MAKES 8 SERVINGS

Herbsaint is a New Orleans Liqueur, it has an anise or licorice flavor. If you cannot find it Pernod is a good substitute.

1- In heavy soup pot heat Olive Oil, add diced Onions, Celery. Sauté for 8-10 minutes.

2- Add Garlic and stir in Flour. Add a dash of Nutmeg.

3- Add Chicken Stock and simmer for 15-20 minutes. Add cleaned Spinach and cook for 5 more minutes.

4- Pour Spinach mixture into a bowl. Taking a quarter of the mixture at a time, put into food processor and puree.

5- Pour pureed Spinach mixture back into the soup pot.

6- Add Cream, Herbsaint Liqueur or Pernod. Add Salt and Cayenne Pepper. Simmer for 20-30 minutes.

7- The Soup will seem thick, but when you add the Oysters it thins the Soup quite a bit.

8- Get Soup very hot just before serving. Add Oysters and simmer for 10 minutes.

9- Garnish Soup with Grated Romano Cheese on top.

Variations on the dish-

If you are not a fan of Oysters, you can substitute Rock Shrimp or Crab Meat. The Crab Meat will not thin the Soup like the Oysters or Shrimp. If you add Crab Meat you may need to add a little Milk to thin the Soup.

Ingredients for Oyster Rockefeller Soup

- 2 tbls.   Olive Oil
- 1 cup   Diced Onion
- 1 cup   Diced Celery
- 1 tbls.   Minced Garlic
- 3 tbls.   Flour
- 1 dash   Nutmeg
- 1 1/2 lbs. Fresh Spinach
- 1 cup   Chicken Stock
- 1 qt.   Cream
- 1/4 cup   Herbsaint or Pernod
- 1 teas.   Salt
- 1/8 teas.   Cayenne
- 1 pint   Fresh Shucked Gulf or East Coast Oysters
- 1 cup   Fresh Grated Romano Cheese

THREE LAYER APPLE PIE WITH PECAN CRUST

MAKES 12 SERVINGS
You will need a 10 inch spring form pan. Spray with Oil.

To make Crust
1- In food processor add Flour, Pecans and Sugar. Pulse a few seconds.

2- Cut Margarine and Butter into pieces and add to food processor. Pulse a few seconds. Margarine and Butter should be the size of green peas.

3- Add a little Ice Water at a time to bind.

4- Press Dough into spring form pan evenly on bottom and sides. Bake at 350 degrees for 10 minutes.

To make Cream Cheese Layer
1- Soften Cream Cheese.

2- Beat Eggs with Sugar until pale yellow. Add in Softened Cream Cheese and beat until smooth.

3- Pour into bottom of Crust and bake at 350 degrees for 30 minutes.

To make Apple Layer
1- Peel, core and slice Apples.

2- Sauté Apples in Butter, Cinnamon and Brown Sugar.

3- Dissolve Corn Starch with some of the liquid from the Apples. Stir back into Apples.

4- Cool for a few minutes then pour on top of Cream Cheese Layer.

To make Topping Layer
1- In food processor add Flour, Brown Sugar and Pecans. Pulse for a few seconds.

2- Cut Butter into pieces. Add to Flour mixture and pulse until crumbly.

3- Sprinkle on top of Apple Layer and bake at 350 degrees for 30 minutes.

Let cool at least 15-20 minutes before removing from pan.

Ingredients for Pecan Crust

- 2 cups — Flour
- 1 cup — Pecans
- 3 teas. — Sugar
- 1 stick — Margarine
- 1/2 stick — Butter
- A few tbls. — Ice Water

Ingredients for Cream Cheese Layer

- 8 oz. — Cream Cheese
- 4 — Eggs
- 1/2 cup — Sugar

Ingredients for Apple Layer

- 5 — Granny Smith Apples
- 1/2 stick — Butter
- 1 cup — Brown Sugar
- 2 tbls. — Corn Starch
- 1 teas. — Cinnamon

Ingredients for Topping Layer

- 1 — Stick of Butter
- 1/2 cup — Brown Sugar
- 1/4 cup — Flour
- 1/2 cup — Pecans

Pumpkin Chili in the Garden

Menu

Roasted Pumpkin Chili
Spicy Corn Topping

Sausages in Spiced Beer
with Mustard

Roasted Peppers & Onions

Cinnamon Candied Apples

Leaf Sugar Cookies

ROASTED PUMPKIN CHILI

MAKES 8 SERVINGS
To Roast Pumpkin (Squash may be used)
1- Preheat oven to 400 degrees.

2- Cut Yams in half and cut Pumpkin into eighths. Leave New Potatoes and Jalapenos and Garlic Cloves whole.

3- Place on large baking sheet. Salt and Pepper the tops and drizzle just a touch of Olive Oil on top of the Pumpkin. Place in hot oven. Roast for 30 minutes then remove the Jalapenos and Garlic Cloves. Let cool and cut Jalapeno into strips removing the seeds. Cut Garlic into quarters.

4- Continue to roast but every ten minutes, using a fork, check for doneness of Vegetables. They should be firm but the fork should go through without excessive effort.

5- Let Vegetables cool. Peel the Yams and Pumpkin and cut into 3/4 inch cubes. Leave the skin on the Potatoes and dice into 1/2 inch cubes.

To Complete Chili
1- In 4 qt. pot add Olive Oil and heat over medium heat.
2- Dice Zucchini into 3/4 inch cubes and set aside.
3- Add diced Onion and Peppers to hot Oil and sauté for two minutes to brown. Add diced Zucchini and sauté for one minute.
4- Add Roasted Vegetables, Garlic and Jalapenos.
5- Add cooked Pinto Beans, Rotel Tomatoes and Diced Tomatoes.
6- Stir in Chili Powder and stir well. Taste and adjust Salt, begin with 1/2 teaspoon. Simmer Chili for 30 minutes.
To Serve Chili
1- Serve Chili in shallow soup bowls.
2- Top with Sour Cream.
3- Top Chili and Sour Cream with Spicy Corn.

Ingredients for Roasted Pumpkin Chili

- 2 tbls.   Olive Oil
- 1 medium   Diced Onion
- 1 medium   Diced Sweet Red Pepper
- 2   Fresh Jalapenos
- 1 lb.   Yams
- 1 lb.   Pumpkin or Squash
- 4   Small New Red Potato
- 8   Garlic Cloves
- 2   Zucchini
- 2 cups   Cooked Pinto Beans
- 2   10 oz. cans Rotel Tomatoes
- 1   12 oz. can Diced Tomatoes
- 2 tbls.   Ground Chili Powder
- •   Salt and Pepper

SPICY CORN TOPPING

Ingredients for Spicy Corn Topping

- 2   Ears of Yellow Corn
- 1   Mrs. Renfro's Spicy Green Salsa (16 oz. jar) or any brand you like of spicy Salsa Verde- My recipe is on page 46
- •   Sour Cream is Optional

MAKES 3 CUPS

1- Shuck yellow Corn and remove kernels with a sharp knife.
2- Get a cast iron skillet or sauté pan very hot.
3- Place Corn Kernels into skillet and brown. Use a metal spatula to move the Corn around to roast the Corn Kernels.
4- Mix roasted Corn Kernels with Green Salsa.
5- Serve on top of Roasted Pumpkin Chili.

Sausages in Spiced Beer with Mustard

MAKES 8 SERVINGS

1- Get iron skillet hot. Place Sausages into hot skillet and brown on all sides.

2- Add Beer, Fennel Seeds and Mustard Seeds, simmer over medium heat until Sausages are done, about 20-25 minutes.

3- Heat Buns and put Mustards in small serving bowls.

4- Serve Sausages in shallow bowl with any of the liquid that is left.

5- Serve with warm Buns, Mustards and Roasted Peppers and Onions.

Ingredients for Sausage in Spiced Beer

- 4 — Bratwurst or Garlic Sausage
- 4 — Hot Italian Sausage
- 1/2 teas. — Fennel Seeds
- 1/2 teas. — Mustard Seeds
- 2 — 12 oz. Beers
- 8 — Poboy or Hoagie Buns
- 4 oz. — Brown Mustard
- 4 oz. — Whole Grain Mustard

Ingredients for Roasted Peppers and Onions

- 2 tbls. — Olive Oil
- 1 — Medium Onion
- 1 — Red Bell Pepper
- 1 — Yellow Bell Pepper
- 1 tbls. — Whole Grain Mustard
- 1/2 teas. — Black Pepper

Roasted Peppers & Onions

MAKES 8 SERVINGS

1- Peel Onion and cut in half. Slice into thin half rounds.

2- Cut Peppers in half and remove seeds. Cut into 1/4 inch strips.

3- In skillet pour in Olive Oil and get Oil hot. Then add Onions and cook for 3 minutes before adding Peppers. Continue to cook until Onions and Peppers are browning and soft.

4- Add Mustard and Pepper and cook for 1 minute more.

5- Serve in a bowl next to the Sausages.

CINNAMON CANDIED APPLES

MAKES 8 SERVINGS
You will need a Candy Thermometer.

1- Wash and dry Apples. Push Popsicle sticks in the bottom of the Apple.

2- Cover a cookie sheet with wax paper.

3- In heavy sauce pan add Sugar, White Karo Syrup and Water. Bring to a boil then turn down to medium heat. Cook until nearly 300 degrees.

4- Drop a little Sugar Syrup into a glass of water to see if Sugar is at hard ball stage. It will be brittle when the water cools it down. Now stir in Cinnamon and Red Food Coloring.

5- Dip each Apple in mixture and coat well. Place down on wax paper and let cool.

6- These are best served within a day.

Ingredients for Cinnamon Candied Apples

•	8	McIntosh Apples
•	8	Popsicle Sticks
•	2 cups	Sugar
•	1/2 cup	White Karo Syrup
•	3/4 cup	Water
•	1/8 teas.	Cinnamon
•	8 drops	Red Food Coloring

LEAF SUGAR COOKIES

Ingredients for Leaf Sugar Cookies

•	1/2 cup	Butter
•	3/4 cup	Sugar
•	1	Egg
•	2 tbls.	Milk
•	1 teas.	Vanilla
•	2 teas.	Grated Lemon Rind
•	2 1/2 cups	Flour
•	1 teas.	Baking Powder
•	1	Egg White
•		Yellow, Orange and Red Decorative Cookie Sugar

MAKES 3 DOZEN
You will need a Leaf shaped Cookie Cutter.

1- In mixing bowl cream Butter, Sugar, Egg, Milk, Vanilla and Lemon Rind.

2- Sift the Flour and Baking Powder.

3- Mix in the Flour mixture to make a stiff but workable Dough.

4- Refrigerate at least 6 hours. Divide in half and roll Dough out, on a floured surface, to less than a 1/4 inch thick.

5- Cut into leaf shapes and place on Oiled baking sheet.

6- Brush with Egg White and decorate with Yellow, Orange and Red Sugar to look like a Fall Leaves.

7- Bake at 375 degrees for 8 minutes. Let cool on rack and serve.

Fall Cooking Class
Menu

Creole Corn Crab Bisque

Wilted Lettuce Salad with
Andouille Vinaigrette and Fried Onions

Roast Duck
Fig & Lemon Preserves

Corn Pudding Stuffed
with Mustard Greens

Coffee Profiteroles with
Bitter Sweet Chocolate Sauce

CREOLE CORN-CRAB BISQUE

MAKES 8 SERVINGS
To make Dark Roux - in heavy iron skillet brown equal amounts of Oil and Flour and stir until chocolate brown.

1- In large soup pot add Margarine first and heat for a few minutes. Add Onion and Bell Pepper. Sauté for 4 minutes.

2- Add Green Onion, Garlic, Basil, Corn Puree. Sauté for 2 minutes.

3- Add Tomato Puree, Dark Roux and Shell Fish Stock. Cook over medium heat and stir until Roux is dissolved.

4- Add half of a Lemon and 1/2 tbls. of Cajun Seasoning, let cook over medium heat for 20 minutes.

5- Remove Lemon and taste Bisque before adding more Cajun Seasoning.

6- Add Fresh Corn Kernels and Crab Meat and simmer for another 20 minutes before serving.

Crawfish or Shrimp may be used instead of Crabmeat.

Stock may be made by using "Gumbo Crabs", these are even available in the frozen section of Wal-Mart.

Ingredients for Creole Corn Crab Bisque

- 3 tbls.   Margarine
- 1 cup   Pureed Onion
- 3/4 cup   Pureed Bell Pepper
- 1/2 cup   Minced Green Onion
- 2 tbls.   Minced Garlic
- 2 tbls.   Minced Fresh Basil
- 1 cup   Fresh Corn Puree
- 2 cups   Tomato Puree (canned)
- 1/2 cup   Dark Roux
- 4 cups   Shell Fish Stock
- 1/2   Lemon
- 1 tbls.   Cajun Seasoning
- 1 cup   Fresh Corn Kernels
- 1 lb.   Crab Meat

Diced Green Onion for Garnish

WILTED LETTUCE SALAD WITH ANDOUILLE VINAIGRETTE

MAKES 8 SERVINGS
This is made in one skillet and served immediately.

1- Get skillet hot and add diced Andouille. Brown evenly and add minced Shallot.

2- Add Brown Sugar, Mustard and Cider Vinegar. Stir until Sugar dissolves.

3- Add Olive Oil and stir again.

4- Add Red Chard and stir until Chard stems begin to soften.

5- Stir in Frisee and cook for 30 seconds.

6- Place Wilted Salad on salad plates and top with Fried Onions and serve immediately.

Ingredients for Wilted Lettuce Salad with Andouille Vinaigrette	
• 1/2 lb.	Diced Andouille
• 1	Minced Shallot
• 2 tbls.	Brown Sugar
• 4 tbls.	Dijon Mustard
• 4 tbls.	Cider Vinegar
• 3 tbls.	Olive Oil
• 1 lb.	Frisee
• 1/2 lb.	Red Chard

Ingredients for Fried Onions	
• 1 qt.	Fry Oil
• 2	White Onions
• 2	Egg Yolks
• 1 cup	Cold Water
• 1 cup	Flour
•	Salt and Pepper

FRIED ONIONS

MAKES 8 SERVINGS
In deep fryer heat Oil to 350 degrees.

1- Peel Onion and cut in half then slice 1/4 inch thick. Separate Onion strips.

2- In mixing bowl beat Egg Yolks with fork and add to very Cold Water. Continue to use the fork and stir in the Flour. The Batter will be slightly lumpy. Add a little Salt and Pepper.

3- Dip Onion pieces into Batter and drop into hot Oil. Fry until golden brown.

4- Top each Salad with Fried Onion Strips.

CORN PUDDING STUFFED WITH MUSTARD GREENS

MAKES 8 SERVINGS

You will need 8 buttered Pyrex Custard Cups or baking dish. Preheat oven to 350 degrees.

1- In large sauté pan melt Butter, add Onion, Celery, Bell Pepper and cook until soft.

2- Add Garlic, Sage, Basil, Black Pepper, Crushed Red Pepper. Cook for one minute more.

3- Remove from heat and pour into a large mixing bowl. Add crumbled Cornbread and stir. Add in Cream.

4- In small bowl beat Eggs well before adding to Cornbread mixture. Stir Eggs in and make sure mixture is well mixed.

5- Fill buttered baking dishes half full with Corn Pudding mixture.

6- Then put two tablespoons of cooked chopped Mustard Greens.

7- Add more Corn Pudding mixture but do not fill to the top.

8- Place in Baking dish with 1/2 inch of water, cover with foil and bake at 350 degrees for 50-60 minutes. Should be firm to the touch in the middle of each dish.

9- Turn out for individual servings. These may be made ahead and re-heated.

Ingredients for Corn Pudding stuffed with Mustard Greens

- 1/4 lb.   Butter
- 1 cup   Diced Onion
- 1 cup   Diced Celery
- 1/2 cup   Diced Red Pepper
- 2 tbls.   Garlic
- 1/8 teas.   Sage
- 1/8 teas.   Basil
- 1/2 teas.   Black Pepper
- 1/8 teas.   Crushed Red Pepper
- 3 cups   Crumbled Cornbread
- 1 cup   Cream
- 4   Eggs
- 2 cups   Cooked Mustard Greens

Ingredients for Fig and Lemon Preserves

- 1 lb.   Dry Figs
- 1/2 cup   Brandy
- 4   Lemons
- 2 lbs.   Sugar

FIG AND LEMON PRESERVES

1- Soak Dry Figs in Brandy for one hour.

2- Slice Lemon as thin as possible and remove any seeds that are visible.

3- Place Lemons and Brandy Soaked Figs in a large heavy saucepan and cover with the 2 lbs. of Sugar. Cook slowly until Sugar is melted.

4- Continue to cook for at least an hour. It may take up to 90 minutes. The lemons should be caramelized.

How to Cook
Duck

I find it essential to prepare Duck properly you have to cook the Breast separate from the Leg and Thigh. This is time consuming but it takes some time proven French Methods and provides such a well prepared Duck that you have to do little else to compliment it.

TO PREPARE YOUR DUCKS - REMOVE THE LEG AND THIGHS AND THE BREASTS.

1- Turn the Duck on its Breast and cut off the Wings where they join the body. Be careful not to cut into the Breast meat.

2- Turn the Duck on its back and pull one Thigh forward and out. Cut through the skin between the Thigh and the Breast, keeping the knife blade against the Thigh. Follow the strip of fat that lies under the skin and leads along the side of the Thigh down to the back.

3- Fold the Thigh back and with your thumb against the base of the Thigh, snap the Thigh out of the joint.

4- Slide your knife along the side of the Duck where the Thigh meat attaches to the back. Follow the contours of the backbone, leaving the meat attached to the Thigh. Detach the Thigh. Repeat to cut off the other Leg.

5- Turn the Duck on its back. Cut along one side of the Breast bone, keeping the knife flush against the bone, until you have detached the Breast along the entire length of the backbone. Leave the skin on, you are removing it intact.

6- Peel the Breast back, away from the bone, with your fingers and slide the knife under the wishbone, detaching it from the Breast.

7- Continue sliding the knife against the Breast bone, keeping the knife against the bone so you don't cut into the Breast meat until you completely detach the boneless Breast.

8- Place the Breast skin side down on the cutting board and cut away excess skin and fat. Repeat with the other Breast.

TO COOK THE LEGS AND THIGHS (this is a modified Confit Recipe, but it makes the Duck so tender, it is worth the effort).

1- Preheat the oven to 325°F, Salt and Pepper the four Legs and Thighs.

2- Place the Legs and Thighs in a dish deep enough to cover them with Oil.

3- Add the Garlic Cloves, Thyme and Bay leaves.

4- Bake until the Garlic Cloves have turned a deep golden color, which will take 2 to 2-1/2 hours.

The Duck is fully cooked, now you just drain off the excess Oil.

5- Place a skillet over medium heat. Place the Legs and Thighs and cook long enough for the Skin to become crispy and nicely browned, approx. 12-14 minutes.

TO COOK THE BREASTS

1- Season Duck Breast with Garlic, Kosher Salt and Cracked Black Pepper.

2- Place heavy skillet over medium heat.

3- Place Duck Breast Skin side down. Slowly cook until Skin is thin and crisp. This takes at least 30 minutes. If the Skin is browning too fast, your heat is too high. The idea is to render the Fat but not over cook the Breast. I often do this hours in advance. The Duck Breast will stay rare on the uncooked side.

4- When ready to serve, place Duck Breast Skin side up and quickly heat the uncooked side. You should have your Duck Breasts a perfect medium rare. If you like it cooked more, it only takes a few minutes to cook with the Skin side up.

Ingredients for Roast Duck

- 2   Whole Long Island Ducklings (provides 4 Breasts and 4 Thighs and Legs)

Ingredients for Confit Duck Legs

- 3 tbls.   Kosher Salt
- 2 tbls.   Black Pepper
- 8   Garlic Cloves
- 4 cups   Oil (if you don't take the time to render the Duck Fat- just use vegetable oil)
- 4 sprigs   Fresh Thyme (or 1 tbls. dry Thyme)
- 3   Bay leaves

Ingredients to Season Duck Breasts

- 1 tbls.   Kosher Salt
- 1 tbls.   Cracked Black Pepper
- 2 tbls.   Minced Garlic

PROFITEROLES FILLED WITH COFFEE ICE CREAM

MAKES 24 PROFITEROLES
You will need two Oiled baking sheets. Preheat oven to 400 degrees.

1- In medium sauce pan add the Water and Butter, bring to a boil. While the Water is heating, sift the Flour.

2- Right when the Water boils, turn it off and add the Flour and beat with a wooden spoon. This mixture should pull from the sides. Place the Dough over the heat for just a few more seconds, then pull off the heat again.

3- Beat in two Eggs, using vigorous strokes. Add the other Eggs one at a time.

4- Let Dough rest for 5-10 minutes. Then spoon or pipe into 2 inch balls. Space 3 inches apart on baking sheet.

5- Bake at 400 degrees for 20 minutes, then turn off the oven, slightly open the oven door and leave in oven for another 5-7 minutes.

6- Remove and place on wire rack to cool. Pierce each one with a small paring knife to let out the steam so the Profiteroles stay firm.

7- When ready to serve, cut and fill with Coffee Ice Cream, place three in a dessert bowl and lace with Bitter-Sweet Chocolate Sauce. Serve immediately.

Ingredients for Profiteroles	
• 1 cup	Flour
• 3/4 cup	Water
• 1/2 cup	Butter
• 4	Eggs
• 1 qt.	Coffee Ice Cream

BITTER-SWEET CHOCOLATE SAUCE

MAKES 8 SERVINGS

1- In small sauce pan heat Cream and Brandy.

2- Add Chocolate. Over very low heat, stir until Chocolate melts and makes a thick Chocolate Sauce.

3- If the Sauce is too thin add another ounce of Chocolate.

Ingredients for Bitter-Sweet Chocolate Sauce	
• 12 oz.	Bitter-Sweet Chocolate
• 3/4 cup	Cream
• 1 oz.	Brandy

Poker Night Gumbo

Menu

Hearts of Palm
Butter Lettuce and Romaine
with Mustard Vinaigrette

Chicken & Andouille Gumbo

Seafood Gumbo

Assorted Breads with
Roasted Red Pepper Butter

Chocolate Orange
Bread Pudding
with Caramelized Sugar Sauce

Hearts of Palm
Butter Lettuce and Romaine
With Mustard Vinaigrette

MAKES 12 SERVINGS

1- Wash Lettuce and spin dry with a salad spinner.

2- Cut Hearts of Palm at an angle about half inch thick.

3- In blender add Shallots, Dijon Mustard, Tarragon Vinegar, Salt and Sugar and puree.

4- Slowly add Olive Oil to emulsify.

5- In Salad Bowl add Lettuce and Hearts of Palm, add a little dressing at a time and toss until Lettuce is lightly coated with Dressing.

6- Garnish with Mild or Spicy Peppadew Peppers that have been cut in Quarters.

Ingredients for Hearts of Lettuce With Mustard Vinaigrette

•	12 oz.	Hearts of Butter Lettuce
•	1 lb.	Hearts of Romaine
•	2 cups	Heart of Palm
•	12	Peppadew Peppers

Ingredients for Mustard Vinaigrette

•	2	Shallots
•	3 tbls.	Dijon Mustard
•	1/4 cup	Tarragon Vinegar
•	1/2 cup	Olive Oil
•	1 teas.	Salt
•	2 teas.	Sugar

CHICKEN-ANDOUILLE GUMBO
SEAFOOD GUMBO

MAKES 2 GALLONS OF GUMBO

Do not let this quantity scare you...Gumbo freezes well. If you are going to go to the trouble to make a good Gumbo, you should have some for later. If you want to cut this recipe in half just divide everything in half.

1- In 10 quart soup pot or gumbo pot add a little Oil or margarine and sauté Onion, Celery and Bell Pepper.

2- Add Garlic Powder, Basil, Thyme and File. Then add Dark Roux and stir until it is blended with the Vegetables.

3- Add the Stock and stir until the Roux is dissolved in the Stock.

4- Add Diced Tomatoes and Okra. Then add Cajun Seasoning (some brands are more salty than others so be careful and hold some back to make sure it is not over-salted)

5- Cook Gumbo over medium heat for ninety minutes.

6- Then divide the Gumbo Base into two pots. Half for Chicken-Andouille Gumbo and the other for Seafood Gumbo.

7- For the Chicken Gumbo add the Andouille and Chicken and cook for another 20 minutes. It is best to let this sit for one hour and then reheat to serve.

8- For the Seafood add the Gumbo Crabs and simmer for 30 minutes.

9- Bring the Seafood Gumbo to a boil then add the Crabmeat and Shrimp and turn off. Let stand for one hour then reheat to serve.

Serve with Rice in the center of the bowl or plain.

Ingredients for Double Batch of Gumbo

To make Chicken-Andouille and Seafood, you will divide your Gumbo Base and add the additional ingredients after 90 minutes.

- 3 cups   Chopped Onion
- 3 cups   Chopped Bell Pepper
- 3 cups   Chopped Celery
- 1 tbls.   Garlic Powder
- 1 tbls.   Basil (dry)
- 1 teas.   Thyme (dry)
- 4 tbls.   Gumbo File
- 1 1/2 cups   Dark Roux (page 236)
- 6 quarts   Chicken Stock
- 4 cups   Canned Diced Tomatoes
- 8 cups   Frozen Okra
- 2 tbls.   Cajun Seasoning
- 1 tbls.   Salt

For Chicken-Andouille Gumbo
- 3 cups   Diced Andouille Sausage
- 6 cups   Diced cooked Chicken

I often use Rotisserie Chickens from the grocery store. I like using white and dark meat and they have good flavor for soups and gumbos.

For Seafood Gumbo
- 4   Gumbo Crabs

(these are usually in the frozen food section, Blue Crabs that have been cleaned and the hard shell removed).

- 2 cups   Crab Meat or Shelled Crab Claws
- 6 cups   Shrimp- peeled and deveined

Optional-
- 1 pint   East Coast Oysters

I do not recommend Pacific Oysters- they are not to my taste.
I often add Andouille to my Seafood Gumbo, I like the smoky flavor.

149

Chocolate-Orange Bread Pudding

MAKES 12 INDIVIDUAL SERVINGS

1- Heat Cream in a double boiler.

2- Add Chocolate to Cream.

3- Whip Egg Yolks and Sugar in mixer until pale yellow.

4- Add Egg Yolks to Chocolate mixture along with Orange Extract.

5- Stir constantly until ribbon stage (about 30 minutes).

6- Dice four cups of Brioche or White Bread without crust and add to Pudding mixture.

7- Spray coffee cups with Spray Oil and fill 3/4 full with Pudding mixture.

8- Bake in water bath at 400 degrees for 55 minutes.

Ingredients for Chocolate-Orange Bread Pudding

•	12 oz.	Semi-Sweet Chocolate
•	3 cups	Cream
•	12 each	Egg Yolks
•	1 cup	Sugar
•	1 teas.	Orange Extract
•	1/4 cup	Grated Orange Zest
•	4 cups	Small cubes of Brioche or White Bread

Caramelized Sugar Sauce

Ingredients for Caramelized Sugar Sauce

•	1/2 cup	Water
•	1 1/2 cups	Sugar

MAKES 2 CUPS

1- In sauce pan or sauté pan add Sugar and Water.

2- Boil Syrup rapidly until the color begins to change to brown.

3- Lower the heat and tilt the pan back and forth a couple of times. When the Syrup is a nice caramel color immediately remove from heat and place bottom of pan in ice water.

4- Keep Sauce at room temperature until serving.

Flavored Butters

Ingredients for Flavored Butters

•	1 lb.	Butter
•	1/4 cup	Dried Red Pepper

Other Variations

•	1 lb.	Butter
•	1/4 cup	Sun Dried Tomato

Or

•	1 lb.	Butter
•	1/2 cup	Orange Marmalade
•	1 tbls.	Cracked Black Pepper

Fall Dinner

Menu

Salad with Warm Cheeses

Regina's Butter Biscuits

Pork Roast with Turnips

Yellow Squash with Peppered Walnuts

Scalloped Yams

Sour Cherry Clafouti

Regina's Butter Biscuits

1- Start with Flour, Baking Powder and Sugar and blend it well (on low speed unless you want to be covered in it!), about 10 seconds with an electric mixer or about 20 strokes by hand.

2- Cut chilled Margarine and Butter into small cubes. The Butter is harder than the Margarine so cut it into smaller pieces, about half an inch. Cut the Margarine slightly larger. Butter gives the Biscuits richness and Margarine makes them flaky. Most everyone uses Crisco or lard, but I use Margarine and Butter because I like the flavor and texture.

Ingredients for Regina's Butter Biscuits

- 4 cups — Flour
- ¼ cup — Baking Powder
- ¼ cup — Sugar
- ¾ pound — Margarine (salted)
- ¼ pound — Butter (salted)
- 1¾ cups — Buttermilk

3- Add the Butter and Margarine to the dry ingredients and blend it quickly to coat the pieces in the Flour mixture. Never blend it into tiny pieces, keep at least size of a nickel until rolling into layers.

4- Once the Butter and Margarine pieces are coated gently, pour the Buttermilk into the bowl and blend for about 10 seconds with a mixer or until a sticky Dough forms. Be careful not to over mix. An over-mixed Biscuit isn't flaky, it becomes like a regular Biscuit, like somebody else's Biscuit, not mine.

5- Liberally Flour the work surface and turn the Dough out onto it, patting it gently into a ball. You should see nickel size pieces of Butter and Margarine in the Dough. The marbling is very important.

6- Use a rolling pin to roll the Dough into a rectangle about ¾-inch thick. Fold the dough in half, bringing the two short ends together, turn it a half turn, and roll it again. Repeat the fold, turn and roll a total of four times. With baking versus cooking, it's a science, not a feeling, there's a huge difference whether you turn the Dough three or four times. On the fourth (and final) roll, use the pin to roll the Dough to a thickness of approximately ½-inch.

7- Cut the Biscuits using a 2- or 3-inch round Biscuit cutter (I prefer 2-inch). The Dough should be layered with Butter and Margarine, if any large pieces remain more than the size of a dime, it should be pulled out, cut or broken into smaller pieces, and pressed back into the Dough. After the Biscuits have been cut, any remnants of Dough should not be rerolled to make more Biscuits, because that will compromise the flakiness of the final product. I take leftover Biscuit Dough - I'm such a perfectionist about layering - and put it into a Ziploc and freeze it for later. I roll it in Sugar and use it for Fruit Shortbreads and Cobblers.

8- Bake the Biscuits at 375 degrees for 20-24 minutes or until golden brown.

Additional Notes: You can bake them in Muffin tins for perfect round Biscuits.
Always make certain your baking sheet has sides so the Butter does not run out into the oven.
The Biscuit Dough freezes well. Freeze on a cookie sheet then transfer to Ziploc bags.
Defrost frozen Biscuits for 15 minutes before baking.

Regina's Butter Biscuits

SALAD WITH WARM CHEESES

MAKES 4 SERVINGS
You will need a nonstick Teflon skillet.

1- Toss Salad Greens with Mustard Vinaigrette.

2- Arrange Salad on individual salad plates.

3- In a nonstick skillet place Brie, Chevre and Blue Cheeses with a 2 inch space in between each.

4- Place the skillet under the broiler of your oven to melt Cheeses. Melt the Cheeses, but do not brown.

5- With a rubber spatula evenly distribute each type of Cheese on to the top of each Salad.

6- Garnish with Toasted French Bread Rounds

Ingredients for Salad with Warm Cheeses

•	3 cups	Mixed Salad Greens
•	3 oz.	Mustard Vinaigrette (recipe on page 148)
•	3 oz.	Brie Cheese
•	3 oz.	Chevre Cheese
•	3 oz.	Blue Cheese
•	8	Toasted French Bread Rounds

PEPPERED WALNUTS

MAKES 4 SERVINGS
You will need a piece of wax paper on a baking sheet.

1- In heavy cast iron skillet add Walnuts and Sugar.

2- Over medium heat stir Sugar and Walnuts until Sugar begins to dissolve. Stir constantly with a wooden spoon.

3- Add Pepper and Salt.

4- After Sugar has melted and Walnuts are well coated, pour the Peppered Walnuts out onto wax paper. Separate the Walnuts as much as possible with the wooden spoon.

Ingredients for Peppered Walnuts

•	2 cups	Walnut Halves
•	1/2 cup	Sugar
•	2 teas.	Cracked Black Pepper
•	1/2 teas.	Salt

Pork Roast with Turnips

MAKES 4 SERVINGS
This cut of Pork is nothing you will find sitting on display. Go to the extra trouble to have your meat cut special for this dish.
Preheat oven to 450 degrees.

1- Place Pork Rib Roast in roasting pan.

2- Season Roast with Mustard, Garlic, Pepper and Salt.

3- Peel and cut Turnips into quarters. Blanch Turnips in boiling water for 6 minutes. Drain off water.

4- Arrange Turnips around Pork Roast.

5- Place Pork Roast and Turnips into 450 degree oven for 15 minutes.

6- Add White Wine.

7- Turn oven down to 350 for another 12-15 minutes. Pork should be cooked medium or 140 degrees.

8- Slice and serve Pork Rib Chop with pan drippings drizzled over each Chop and garnish with Roasted Turnip.

Ingredients for Pork Roast with Turnips

- 2 1/2 lb.　　4 Chop Center Cut Pork Rib Roast
- 2 tbls.　　Mustard
- 2 tbls.　　Minced Garlic
- 1 tbls.　　Black Pepper
- 2 teas.　　Salt
- 1/2 cup　　White Wine
- 4　　Turnips

Yellow Squash with Peppered Walnuts

Ingredients for Yellow Squash with Peppered Walnuts

- 3　　Yellow Squash
- 2 tbls.　　Butter
- 1/4 teas.　　Salt
- 1 cup　　Peppered Walnuts

MAKES 4 SERVINGS

1- Wash and dry Yellow Squash. Cut in half length-wise and then cut into half rounds.

2- Place sauté pan over high heat, add Butter and let melt.

3- Add Squash right away and sauté for 2 minutes or until Squash is soft.

4- Add Peppered Walnuts (recipe on page 155) and Salt. Stir and serve.

SCALLOPED YAMS

MAKES 4 SERVINGS
You will need a Pyrex or porcelain 9x9 shallow casserole dish sprayed with Oil. Preheat oven to 375 degrees.

1- Peel Yams and slice very thin. It is best to slice using a mandoline or vegetable slicer.

2- In Oiled shallow baking dish arrange sliced Yams.

3- Salt and Pepper each layer.

4- Mix Cream and melted Butter and pour over Yams.

5- Cover with foil and bake for 40 minutes or until Yams are tender.

6- Let rest for 10 minutes before cutting. Cut into squares and serve.

Ingredients for Scalloped Yams

•	2	Large Yams approx. 4 cups of thinly sliced Yams
•	3 tbls.	Cream
•	3 tbls.	Melted Butter
•	1/2 teas.	Salt
•	1/4 teas.	White Pepper

SOUR CHERRY CLAFOUTI

MAKES 4-6 SERVINGS
Pre heat oven to 425 degrees. You will need a 9 inch pie plate. Heat the pie plate in the oven while you are making your batter.

1- Drain all liquid from the canned Sour Cherries and place in glass bowl, add 2/3 cups of Sugar and 1/4 cup of Brandy. This is best when done the day before or at least three hours before you make the Clafouti. You will add the Cherries after the batter has baked for ten minutes.

2- In blender add Eggs, Salt and melted Butter and Half and Half. Blend for a few seconds until smooth. Add the Orange Zest and Cinnamon and blend.

3- Blend in Flour and Powdered Sugar to make a smooth Batter.

4- Place one ounce of Butter in the bottom of the hot pie plate and place in hot oven for five minutes. Remove from oven and add the Batter. Place back into oven for ten minutes more. Remove from oven and reduce the heat to 350 degrees.

5- Now add the Cherries and immediately return Clafouti to oven continue to bake at 350 degrees for 40-45 minutes. The Clafouti should be golden brown on top and bottom.

6- Slice and serve warm, dust with Powdered Sugar and garnish with Orange Zest.

Ingredients for Sour Cherry Clafouti

•	3 cups	Drained Sour Cherries
•	2/3 cup	Sugar
•	1/4 cup	Brandy

It is best to mix the Cherries, Brandy and Sugar three hours before. If you don't have time, then cook the Sugar and Brandy for five minutes before adding to Cherries.

•	3	Eggs
•	1/8 teas.	Salt
•	2 tbls.	Sweet Cream Butter (melted)
•	1 cup	Half and Half
•	2/3 cup	Flour
•	1/4 cup	Powdered Sugar
•	1 tbls.	Orange Zest
•	1/4 teas.	Cinnamon

For Garnish

•	2 tbls.	Powdered Sugar
•	2 tbls.	Orange Zest

Sunday Supper

Menu

Mixed Greens with
Warm Brie & Currants
Sherry Vinaigrette

Braised Beef Ribs

French Bread
& Tomato Stuffing

Green Beans
with Molasses Vinaigrette

Natchez Beignet
with Vanilla Ice Cream and
Warm Praline Sauce

Mixed Greens with Warm Brie & Currants Sherry Vinaigrette

MAKES 8 SERVINGS

1- In blender add Shallots, Vinegar, Sherry, Honey and Salt. Blend for a few seconds. Add Oil slowly to emulsify (or thicken).

2- Slice Baguette into small rounds. Brush with Oil or Butter and toast.

3- Toss Greens in Dressing. Arrange on serving platter leaving the center open. Place the toasted Baguette slices in the center of the Salad.

4- Put Brie in nonstick pan. Place in 400 degree oven for 4-6 minutes.

5- Pour melted Brie over the toasted Baguette slices.

6- Garnish with Currants and serve right away.

Ingredients for Mixed Greens with Warm Brie & Currants

Ingredients for Sherry Vinaigrette

- 1 teas.   Minced Shallot
- 2 tbls.   Cider Vinegar
- 2 tbls.   Dry Sherry
- 1 tbls.   Honey
- 1/2 cup   Salad Oil
- 1/2 teas. Salt

Ingredients for Salad

- 1 lb.   Mixed Baby Greens
- 8 oz.   Brie Cheese
- 1/4 cup   Currants
- 1   French Bread Baguette

French Bread and Tomato Stuffing

MAKES 8 SERVINGS

1- In large pot melt Butter, sauté Onions, Celery and Peppers until soft.

2- Add Garlic, Basil, Thyme and Chicken Stock, simmer for ten minutes, remove from heat.

3- Quarter Roma Tomatoes and place on baking sheet. Sprinkle with Salt and Pepper. Roast in 400 degree oven until they begin to dry and brown.

4- Combine Bread, roasted Tomatoes and cooked Vegetables. Toss all ingredients well to make sure the Vegetables and roasted Tomatoes are evenly distributed.

5- Pour Stuffing into buttered baking dish and bake at 350 degrees for 40 minutes before serving.

This freezes quite well and can be made in advance.

Ingredients for French Bread and Tomato Stuffing

- 2 cups   Chopped Onion
- 2 cups   Chopped Celery
- 1 cup   Chopped Sweet Red Pepper
- 2 tbls.   Minced Garlic
- 1 tbls.   Minced Basil
- 1 tbls.   Fresh Thyme
- 2 lbs.   Fresh Roma Tomatoes
- 1/2 lb.   Butter
- 1 pint   Chicken Stock or Vegetable Stock
- 6 cups   Diced French Bread or Sourdough
-            Salt and Pepper

Green Beans with Molasses Vinaigrette

MAKES 8 SERVINGS

1– Clean and clip Green Beans. Cook for two minutes in salted, boiling water.

2– In blender puree Shallot, add Molasses, Vinegar and Salt.

3– Pour Molasses mixture into a bowl and hand whisk in the Oil. Do not emulsify.

4– Toss Green Beans in Vinaigrette.

This dish is good served hot or cold and may be served over Mixed Baby Greens.

Ingredients for Green Beans with Molasses Vinaigrette		
•	2 lbs.	Green Beans
	Molasses Vinaigrette	
•	1/2 cup	Molasses
•	4 tbls.	Balsamic Vinegar
•	1/2 teas.	Salt
•	1	Shallot
•	1/4 cup	Salad Oil

BRAISED BEEF RIBS

How to make a Dark Roux- the time is worth the effort...the better the roux...the better your dish.

- 1/2 cup oil
- 1 cup flour

In a cast iron skillet, heat Oil over medium heat until just smoking. Whisk in Flour, a little at a time and cook, whisking constantly, until Roux becomes smooth and thick. Continue to cook, constantly stirring with a spoon and reaching all over bottom of pan, until Roux darkens to a rich brown nutty color, about 25 minutes. Remove from the heat and put into a metal bowl and it will continue to cook but not burn..it will become a chocolate brown, which I find to be the perfect roux.

Yield: about 1 1/2 cups.

MAKES 6 SERVINGS
Large skillet to brown Meat in
A large roasting pan

1- Place large skillet over medium-high heat to get very hot.

2- Season Short ribs with Kosher Salt, Cracked Black Pepper and Garlic Powder.

3- Brown meat on both sides and place in Roasting Pan.

4- After browning Meat add 2 cups of Water to Skillet, two cups of Red Wine and 1/2 cup of Dark Roux. Cook until Roux is dissolved.

5- Pour the liquid mixture from above over browned Meat. Then add the Rosemary and Garlic.

6- Cook for 90 minutes in a 375 degree oven.

7- Remove Ribs and place in baking dish, then pour liquid into a Pyrex dish and put into freezer so the fat will come to the top and you can skim off.

8- After removing the fat, heat the remaining Sauce and pour over the Braised Beef Ribs to serve.

Ingredients for Braised Beef Ribs

Have a butcher cut these for you. You will not normally find these cut this size in the meat counter.

- 6   1 pound Choice or Prime Beef Short Ribs

Kosher Salt, Cracked Black Pepper and Garlic Powder to taste

- 2 cups   Water
- 2 cups   Red Cooking Wine
- 1/4 cup   Dark Roux
- 2   Sprigs of Rosemary
- 3   Cloves of Garlic

PRALINE SAUCE

MAKES 3 CUPS
You will need a large sauce pan (you need a large pan because this mixture foams up while cooking) and a metal wire whisk or wooden spoon.

1- Put all of the ingredients into pan. Turn heat on medium heat.

2- Stir frequently **with a wooden spoon** until Sugar is dissolved.

3- Mixture will begin to foam quite a bit. Stir constantly until foaming stops.

4- The color will begin to caramelize. Continue to cook until it is a smooth caramel color. This whole process takes about 20-30 minutes.

This Sauce will last but will get sugary...just add a bit of hot water and bring to a boil until the sugar crystals dissolve.

Ingredients for Praline Sauce		
• 1 lb.	Sugar
• 1/4 lb.	Butter
• 1/2 teas.	Baking Soda
• 1 cup	Buttermilk
Pecans are optional		

Ingredients for Natchez Beignet		
• 8	Beignets
• 1 qt.	Vanilla Ice Cream
• 3 cups	Praline Sauce
• 1 cup	Chopped Pecans

NATCHEZ BEIGNET

MAKES 6 SERVINGS
You can do the Beignets ahead because by the time you fill the Beignets with Vanilla Ice Cream and pour the hot Praline Sauce you won't be able to tell that they were made ahead.

1- Use half recipe for Beignet Dough. Roll out and fry 8 Beignets.

2- Slice Beignets cutting three sides leaving one side attached.

3- Fill each Beignet with Vanilla Ice Cream and set in shallow dessert bowls.

4- Ladle hot Praline Sauce over each one. Garnish with chopped Pecans and serve immediately.

RECIPE FOR BEIGNET DOUGH PAGE 20

Thanksgiving at Twin Oaks
Menu

Smoked Salmon~Caviar Pies
Sun Dried Tomato~Pesto Torta

Hearts of Romaine with Artichoke Hearts &
Creamy Preserved Lemon Vinaigrette

Smoked Brisket of Beef
Roast Turkey with Creole Gravy

Mushroom~Brioche Sage Dressing

Crawfish~Andouille Cornbread Dressing

Baked Yams with Mango~Cranberry Chutney

Roasted Garlic~Mustard Mashed Potatoes

Creamed Natchez Spinach in a Baked Tomato

Roast Asparagus with Smoked Roma Tomatoes

Yeast Rolls & Butter Biscuits

Blackberry Crème Brule Trifle ~ Pecan Tarts
Sweet Potato Crisps ~ German Chocolate Petits Fours

These are a different variation of the Tortas I did for the Twin Oaks Wedding Menu, but any flavor I seem to come up with and any time of year these are always very well received by guests.

SMOKED SALMON-CAVIAR PIES

MAKES 9 INCH TORTA WHICH SERVES 30

You will need a 9 inch Spring Form Pan, spray well with Spray Oil

1- In large metal bowl add Cream Cheese that has been cut into 1 oz. cubes and Butter that has been cut into 1 oz. cubes and allow to get to room temperature.

2- Once Cream Cheese and Butter has softened, using an Electric Mixer whip the two together, slowly blending in the Sour Cream. This should be blended smoothly with no lumps. Add Garlic Powder and blend until evenly distributed.

3- Chop Hard Boiled Eggs and mix with 1 tbls. Mayonnaise. Use this to line the bottom of the Pan.

4- Take a third of the mixture and spread evenly on top of the Egg Crust.

5- Spread Minced Red Onion on top and add another third of the Cream Cheese Mixture.

6- Sprinkle Capers on top of this layer. Then add the last of the Cream Cheese Mixture. Cover with plastic wrap and refrigerate over night.

7- Loosen the sides and tap gently to un mold. Turn it over on a decorative plate and then top with Smoked Salmon and use Smoked Salmon around the base. Sprinkle the Green Wasabi Caviar on top.

Ingredients for Smoked Salmon-Caviar Pies

32 oz.	Cream Cheese
1/2 lb.	Butter
1 cup	Sour Cream
1 teas	Garlic Powder

Ingredients for Layers

6	Hard Boiled Eggs
1 tbls.	Mayonnaise
1/2 cup	Minced Red Onion
1/4 cup	Capers
1 lb.	Smoked Salmon
4 oz.	Wasabi Caviar

SUNDRIED TOMATO-PESTO TORTA

MAKES 9 INCH TORTA WHICH SERVES 30
You will need a 9 inch Spring Form Pan, spray well with Spray Oil

1- In large metal bowl add Cream Cheese that has been cut into 1 oz. cubes and Butter that has been cut into 1 oz. cubes and allow to get to room temperature.

2- Once Cream Cheese and Butter has softened, using an Electric Mixer whip the two together, slowly blending in the Sour Cream. This should be blended smoothly with no lumps.

3- Place half the Cream Cheese mixture into the Spring Form Pan. Then starting from the center of the Torta, add 1 cup of Sundried Tomato Puree.

4- Add the rest of the Cream Cheese mixture. Cover and refrigerate over night.

Loosen the sides and tap gently to unmold. Turn it over on a decorative plate and then top with Pesto Sauce. Use toasted Pine Nuts to press on the side for decoration.
Serve with Crackers.

Ingredients for Sundried Tomato-Pesto Torta

32 oz.	Cream Cheese
1/2 lb.	Butter
1 cup	Sour Cream
1 cup	Sundried Tomato Puree
1 cup	Pesto
1 cup	Toasted Pine Nuts

HEARTS OF ROMAINE WITH ARTICHOKE HEARTS & CREAMY PRESERVED LEMON VINAIGRETTE

How to Preserve Lemons

1- Score Lemons with a serrated knife from top to bottom (length-wise) every 1/2 inch, all the way around the Lemon.

2- Add Salt and cover with Water (approx. 6 cups should do it).

3- Bring to a boil and them simmer for 20 minutes. Lemons should be soft but not falling apart.

4- Keep Lemons in Salt Water and place in glass bottles for décor or in refrigerator.

I use Preserved Lemons to roast Chicken, I also use it for flavoring to bake Fish.

Preserved Lemon Vinaigrette - this makes more than you need but it keeps well to use again.
In a Blender-

1- Add Preserved Lemon, Shallot and Cider Vinegar. Put the top back on the blender and turn on until the Lemon has been completely pureed.

2- Remove the top and add the Sweetener or Sugar and Dijon Mustard. Put the top back on and puree until all ingredients are evenly blended.

3- If your Blender has the plastic top that you can remove and pour Oil in...that is the best...if not slowly add Oil, mix and repeat.

Ingredients for Preserved Lemons
- 1 dozen   Medium Lemons
- 1/2 cup   Kosher Salt
- 6 cups   Water

Ingredients for Preserved Lemon Vinaigrette
- 1   Preserved Lemon
- 1   Medium Shallot
- 2 teas.   Cider Vinegar
- 2 packets   Equal Sweetener or 4 teas. of Sugar
- 2 tbls.   Dijon Mustard
- 2 cups   Salad Oil

1 Teaspoon of minced Fresh Tarragon is optional...but if you have it, it is a great addition.

Ingredients for Hearts of Romaine-Artichoke Salad
- 3   Hearts of Romaine
- 2 cups   Artichoke Heart
- 1/2 cup   Grated Parmesan or Romano

To Put Salad together-
Clean and dry Romaine Hearts. Slice the Lettuce length-wise and place in a bowl. Add the Artichoke Hearts and enough Lemon Vinaigrette to coat the Lettuce leaves. Toss until Leaves are well coated.
Serve on a chilled platter with the Romaine leaves pointing in the same direction. Sprinkle the Grated Cheese on top and serve.

ROAST TURKEY
CREOLE GRAVY

MAKES 14 SERVINGS

1- Remove Neck and Giblets from Turkey. Rinse Turkey and pat dry. Place Turkey in deep roasting pan. Place Giblets around it, as they will enhance the Gravy flavor. Stuff the cavity with the Garlic, quartered Onion and sliced Celery.

2- Melt the Butter in small sauce pan. Mix together the Butter, Garlic, Herbs, Salt and Pepper and Worcestershire. Rub the Turkey well with this mixture. Take the Anchovy Filets and place on top of the Turkey making a design. *Trust me when I say the Anchovies make this Turkey wonderful! There is no trace of them when it is done.*

3- Add the Water and Wine then cover with two sheets of aluminum foil, one for each side of the roaster, leaving 1/4 inch opening down the center.

Baking options

225 degrees- 7 hours (no need to baste) **or**

350 degrees- 3 hours for 15 lbs. Add 11 minutes per pound after that, baste every hour.

Pierce thigh of Turkey with skewer to check for doneness. Skewer should go in easily and juices should run clear, not pink.

WHILE TURKEY IS COOKING MAKE YOUR ROUX

4- To prepare Roux for Gravy, combine Oil and Flour in a cast iron skillet over medium heat to make a Dark Roux. Stir constantly with a wooden spoon until chocolate brown. Remove from skillet and put into metal bowl. *Once the Roux gets to the proper color it can burn very fast. It is essential that you cool it in another container.*

Remove the Turkey from the oven and place on a platter to rest. Pour Drippings into a sauce pan.

5- Stir in the 4 tbls. of Corn Starch into the two cups of Water and add to the Drippings. Bring to boil and skim off fat. Add 1/4 cup of the Dark Roux and cook slowly for 20 minutes until Gravy thickens. Adjust seasoning with Salt and Pepper. Strain the Gravy and serve.

Ingredients for Roast Turkey	
• 16-18 lb.	Turkey
• 1/2 cup	Butter
• 1/4 cup	Worcestershire Sauce
• 2 tbls.	Minced Garlic
• 2 tbls.	Minced Basil
• 1 tbls.	Minced Thyme
• 2 tbls	Minced Sage
• 2 tbls.	Cracked Black Pepper
• 1 tbls.	Sea Salt
• 2 oz.	Anchovy Filets
• 1 cup	Red Wine
• 1 cup	Water

For Turkey Cavity	
• 4 cloves	Garlic
• 2 medium	Peeled Onions
• 4 ribs	Celery

For Dark Roux	
• 1/4 cup	Vegetable Oil
• 6 tbls.	Flour

For Creole Gravy	
• 4 tbls.	Corn Starch
• 2 cups	Water
• Save the Turkey Drippings.	

MUSHROOM-BRIOCHE SAGE DRESSING

MAKES 12 SERVINGS

1- In large pot melt Butter, sauté Onions, Celery and Peppers until soft.

2- Add Garlic, Sage, Basil and Mushrooms, sauté for a minute.

3- Add Stock, simmer for ten minutes, remove from heat and add Bread. Toss the mixture and make sure the Mushrooms and Vegetables are evenly distributed.

4- Put in buttered or oiled baking dish and bake at 350 degrees for 45-55 minutes before serving.

This freezes quite well and can be made in advance.

If you want this to be sinfully rich I use the fat left over from roasting my Beef Brisket and sauté my Vegetables in it.

Ingredients for Mushroom-Brioche Dressing

• 2 cups	Chopped Onion
• 2 cups	Chopped Celery
• 1 cup	Chopped Sweet Red Pepper
• 2 tbls.	Minced Garlic
• 1 tbls.	Minced Sage
• 1 tbls.	Minced Basil
• 2 lbs.	Assorted Mushrooms
• 1/2 lb.	Butter
• 1 pint	Chicken or Turkey Stock
• 6 cups	Diced Brioche

Brioche is an airy Egg Bread that makes this Dressing better. Use any soft Bread- I often substitute Hot Dog Buns and it works fine.

ROASTED GARLIC & MUSTARD MASHED POTATOES

Ingredients for Roasted Garlic & Mustard Mashed Potatoes

• 2 lbs.	Yukon Gold Potatoes
• 2 lbs.	New Red Potatoes
• 1/2 lb.	Butter (salted)
• 1/2 cup	Buttermilk
• 1 cup	Sour Cream
• 12 cloves	Garlic
• 1 tbls.	Olive Oil
• 1/4 cup	Whole Grain Mustard
•	Salt and White Pepper

I recommend two teaspoons of Salt and a half teaspoon of White Pepper to start and adjust from there.

MAKES 12 SERVINGS

Have a colander in the sink and have an electric hand mixer close by. Even if you have to use an extension cord it is best to whip the Potatoes over a burner on the stove.

You can make these up to two hours ahead of serving time.

1- Wash the Yukon Gold and the Red Potatoes well. Leave the skin on or just peel the Yukon Gold Potatoes.

2- Cut Potatoes in equal size pieces. 2x1 inch cubes work well.

3- Place Potatoes in large pot and cover with cold water and bring to a boil. Turn to medium heat and cook until tender, about 20 minutes.

4- While the Potatoes are cooking place the Garlic Cloves on a small baking sheet and drizzle a touch of Olive Oil over them. Place in 400 degree oven for 8-10 minutes. The Garlic should turn golden brown and be soft to the touch.

5- Combine the Butter and Buttermilk in small sauce pan and warm to melt the Butter. This mixture does not have to be very hot. Add the Sour Cream.

6- When the Potatoes are done, drain them in a colander and cover with a dish towel to help hold in the heat. Let stand for at least 5 minutes. The Potatoes must be dry.

7- Take the pot that the Potatoes cooked in and add the Butter mixture, turn the burner on low.

Pour the Potatoes back into the pot and whip with the electric mixer. Add the Garlic, Mustard and begin to season with Salt and White Pepper. Taste and adjust the seasoning.

Serve immediately or put in glass serving bowl that can be microwaved. Cover with plastic wrap and set aside.

Microwave (with plastic wrap on) for 4-5 minutes.

Remove plastic wrap and serve.

CRAWFISH-ANDOUILLE CORNBREAD DRESSING

MAKES 12 SERVINGS
You will need a buttered Pyrex or baking dish. Preheat oven to 350 degrees.

1- Place large sauté pan over medium heat and add diced Andouille, cook for 5-6 minutes then add Onion, Celery, Bell Pepper and cook until soft.

2- Add Garlic, Sage, Basil, Black Pepper, Crushed Red Pepper. Cook for one minute more.

3- Add Crawfish and cook for two minutes more.

4- Remove from heat and pour into a large mixing bowl. Add crumbled Cornbread and stir.

5- Add in Cream.

6- In small bowl beat Eggs well before adding to Cornbread mixture. Stir Eggs in and make sure mixture is well mixed.

7- Pour into buttered baking dish and bake at 350 degrees for 45-55 minutes. Should be firm to the touch

Ingredients for Crawfish-Andouille Cornbread Dressing	
1 lb.	Diced Andouille Sausage
1 1/2 cup	Diced Onion
1 1/2 cup	Diced Celery
1/2 cup	Diced Red Pepper
3 tbls.	Garlic
3 teas.	Sage
2 teas.	Basil
1 teas.	Black Pepper
1/2 teas.	Crushed Red Pepper
2 lbs.	Crawfish Tail Meat
5 cups	Stale Cornbread
1 1/2 cup	Cream
5	Eggs

The Chapel at Twin Oaks was built by Dr, Whittington in honor of Cornelia Connelly, who lived here in the 1830's. Although the Chapel is rustic and more of a garden ornament the Windows are Tiffany Glass.

BAKED YAMS WITH MANGO-CRANBERRY CHUTNEY

MAKES 12 SERVINGS

1- Rub Yams with Oil and sprinkle with Salt and Pepper.

2- Place on baking sheet and bake for 40-50 minutes. A fork should go through easily when done.

3- Cut in half, top with Sour Cream and Cranberry-Mango Chutney.

MAKES 8 SERVINGS

1- In sauce pan heat Butter, add Onion and Pepper. Sauté for 3 minutes.

2- Add Brown Sugar, Golden Raisins, Currants, Vinegar, Allspice, Cinnamon and Dried Cranberries. Cook for 12-15 minutes.

3- Add Mango and cook for another 3 minutes.

4- Let cool and use as a topping on Baked Yams.

Ingredients for Baked Yams

• 6	Large Yams
• 2 tbls.	Oil
•	Salt and Cracked Pepper
• 8 tbls.	Sour Cream
• 8 tbls.	Cranberry-Mango Chutney

Ingredients for Cranberry-Mango Chutney

• 1 tbls.	Butter
• 1 cup	Chopped Onion
• 1/2 cup	Chopped Red Bell Pepper
• 1/2 cup	Golden Raisins
• 1/4 cup	Dried Currants
• 1/2 cup	Brown Sugar
• 4 tbls.	Cider Vinegar
• 1/8 teas.	Allspice
• 1/8 teas.	Cinnamon
• 1 cup	Dried Cranberries
• 2 cups	Diced Mango

"Natchez Style" Creamed Spinach in Baked Tomato

MAKES 12 SERVINGS

1- With a small paring knife, cut into the center of each Tomato with alternating incision / then \ /\/\/\/\- this will create a star effect for each Tomato half. Then scoop the center of each Tomato half out with a spoon. Place Tomato halves on baking sheet.

2- In sauté pan add 1 tbls. of the 1/4 lb. of Butter and sauté the Baby Spinach Leaves. Drain all the excess liquid.

3- In sauce pan melt the rest of the Butter, add the Cream Cheese, Garlic and Jalapeno. Blend with a wooden spoon until smooth, then add the grated Cheese and cooked Spinach.

4- Spoon Spinach mixture into each Tomato half and bake at 350 degrees for 15-18 minutes.

Ingredients for Creamed Spinach in Baked Tomato

- 6 — Medium size Tomatoes
- 1/4 lb. — Butter
- 12 oz. — Cream Cheese
- 1 cup — Grated Sharp Cheddar
- 1 tbls. — Minced Garlic
- 1 tbls. — Minced Jalapeno
- 2 lb. — Baby Spinach Leaves

Roast Asparagus with Smoked Roma Tomatoes

Ingredients for Roast Asparagus with Smoked Tomatoes

- 2 lbs. — Fresh Asparagus
- 6 — Smoked Roma Tomatoes

  Recipe on page 235
- Mix of 1 tbls. Sea Salt, 1 tbls. of Minced Garlic, 1 tbls. Cracked Black Pepper and 1 teas. Fennel seed.

MAKES 12 SERVINGS

1- Place cast iron skillet over high heat. Get skillet white hot.

2- Cut white bottoms off Asparagus and wash.

3- If the Asparagus are not thinner than a pencil, use a vegetable peeler and peel the bottoms so they are tender.

4- Toss Asparagus in Oil and Spices.

5- Place Asparagus in Cast Iron Skillet. Do not put too many in at once. With metal tongs, turn the Asparagus to roast evenly.

6- Place Roasted Asparagus on serving tray and garnish with Smoked Tomatoes.

YEAST ROLLS

MAKES 2 DOZEN ROLLS
This recipe makes a soft roll for sandwiches.

1- Combine Milk, Water and Margarine in sauce pan. Heat over low heat until mixture is warm (120 degrees). Margarine does not need to melt all the way.

2- Put 3 1/2 cups Flour, Sugar, Salt, Yeast in mixing bowl. Use dough hook on mixer. Turn to speed 2 and mix 15 seconds.

3- Gradually add warm Milk mixture while mixing for another minute.

4- Continue on speed 2, add remaining Flour a half cup at a time, until Dough clings to the dough hook and cleans sides of bowl. This should be about 2 minutes.

5- Turn Dough onto floured cloth or board. Cut into 24 equal pieces. Shape into Rolls.

6- Mix Egg and Water together to make Egg Wash. Brush tops with Egg Wash.

7- Place on Oiled baking sheet and let rise in 90 degree oven for 15 minutes.

8- Turn oven up to 400 degrees and bake for 15 minutes or until golden brown.

RECIPE FOR
BUTTER BISCUITS
ON PAGE 154

Ingredients for Yeast Rolls

- 1 cup   Milk
- 1/2 cup   Water
- 1/4 cup   Margarine
- 4-5 cups   All Purpose Flour
- 3 tbls.   Sugar
- 1 teas.   Salt
- 3 packages Dry Active Yeast

Ingredients for Egg Wash to top Rolls

- 1   Egg
- 1/2 cup   Water

German Chocolate Petits fours

MAKES 24-30 PETITS FOURS

1- Preheat oven to 350 degrees Grease and flour a large cookie sheet with 1 inch sides.

2- In a large bowl, combine the Flour, Sugar, Cocoa, Baking Soda.

3- Make a well in the center and pour in the Eggs, Coffee, Buttermilk and Oil. Mix until smooth, batter will be thin. Pour into prepared pan.

4- Bake in the preheated oven for 35 to 40 minutes, or until a toothpick inserted into the center of the cake comes out clean. Allow to cool.

5- Cut into 2 inch rounds with a biscuit cutter. Place on a sheet pan that has been lined with plastic wrap.

6- Top with German Chocolate Frosting.

7- Drizzle Chocolate Sauce over top.

8- Place in small white baking cups or directly on a decorative cake plate to serve.

* These freeze very well and can be taken out 30 minutes before serving.

MAKES 2 1/2 CUPS OF FROSTING

1- Have a wooden spoon available to stir as ingredient go into a heavy sauce pan. Add Evaporated Milk, Sugar, Egg Yolks and Butter before placing pan over medium heat.

2- Stir frequently and do not get the mixture hot too quickly or your Egg Yolks will curdle. You are basically making a Custard. This takes 10-14 minutes.

3- Add Coconut and Pecans then beat until frosting is cool and thick enough to spread.

Ingredients for Dark Chocolate Sheet Cake

- 2 cups   All Purpose Flour
- 2 cups   White Sugar
- 3/4 cup   Unsweetened Cocoa
- 2 teas.   Baking Soda
- 1 teas.   Baking Powder
- 1/2 teas.   Salt
- 2   Eggs
- 1 cup   Cold Coffee
- 1 cup   Buttermilk
- 1/2 cup   Vegetable Oil

Ingredients for German Chocolate Frosting

- 1 cup   Evaporated Milk
- 1 cup   Sugar
- 3   Egg Yolks
- 1/4 lb.   Butter
- 1 tsp.   Vanilla
- 1 1/3 cup   Baker's Coconut
- 1 cup   Toasted Pecan Pieces

Ingredient for Chocolate Drizzle

- 1 1/2 cups   Dark Chocolate Chips
- 3 tbls.   Water

To Make Chocolate Sauce to Drizzle on top.

Put Chocolate Chips and Water in a microwavable bowl. Cook for 30 seconds at a time. Stir until the Chips are melted and you have a smooth sauce.

If it is too thick add a few drops of Water and stir.

Use a fork to Drizzle on German Chocolate Petits Fours.

SWEET POTATO CRISP

MAKES 2 DOZEN
This can be made in a baking dish and cut into squares or you can use Dutch Ann Tart Shells and make individual tarts. You will need a 9x13 baking dish or two dozen 2 inch Tart shells

Crisp
1- Cut Butter into 1 inch pieces, put in food processor.
2- Add Oats, Flour and Sugar, pulse until it is crumbly, the Butter should be the size of peas.
3- Add Pecans and pulse just two or three times to blend in.
4- In baking pan sprayed with Oil put half the Crisp mixture to line the bottom of the pan and bake at 350 degrees for 8 minutes.

If you are making the individual Tarts you just pour the filling in the Tart Shell, then top with Crisp topping and bake at 350 degrees for 35 minutes.

Filling
1- In metal or glass mixing bowl put all three Eggs and with electric mixer on medium speed, beat until creamy yellow.
2- Add Sweetened Condensed Milk, Cinnamon and Sweet Potatoes. Beat until smooth.
3- Pour into the baking dish with the half baked Crisp bottom.
4- Top with the other half of the Crisp mixture.
5- Bake at 325 degrees for 50-60 minutes. The center should firm like the sides. You can touch to see.
In shallow dessert bowls, ladle Praline Sauce just to cover bottom of bowl. Cut Sweet Potato Crisp into squares and place on top of Sauce. Vanilla Ice Cream is optional.

Ingredients for Sweet Potato Crisp		
Crisp Topping		
•	3/4 lb.	Butter
•	1 1/2 cups	Quick Oats
•	2 cups	Flour
•	2 cups	White Sugar
•	1 cup	Pecans
Sweet Potato Filling		
•	3 cups	Cooked Sweet Potatoes
•	1 can	Sweetened Condensed Milk
•	3	Eggs
•	1 teas.	Cinnamon
•	2 dozen	2 inch Unbaked Tart Shells

PECAN TARTS

MAKES 2 DOZEN

1- In mixing bowl add Eggs and lightly beat.

2- Add Karo Syrup, Brown Sugar and Melted Butter. Beat until smooth. Do not over mix.

3- Add Flour and blend in until smooth.

4- Add Vanilla and blend well.

5- Fold in Chopped or small whole Pecans.

6- Pour into Tart shells. Make sure the bubbles have settled.

7- Bake at 350 degrees for 30-35 minutes.

Ingredients for Pecan Tarts		
•	2	Eggs
•	1 cup	White Karo Syrup
•	1/2 cup	Brown Sugar
•	3 tbls.	Melted Butter
•	2 tbls.	Flour
•	1 teas.	Vanilla
•	1 1/2 cups	Chopped Pecans or small Natchez Pecans
•	2 dozen	3 inch Unbaked Tart Shells

Winter warmth

Coffee Club
Holiday Breakfast at Twin Oaks

Menu

Blackberry Muffins
Cranberry-Orange Muffins

Cinnamon Rolls with Caramel Glaze

Fresh Fruit Compote

Regina's Butter Biscuits
Orange Marmalade Butter
Fig Preserves

Smoked Bacon on Skewers with Brown Sugar

Ham with Pineapple-Pomegranate Glaze

Scrambled Eggs with Smoked Sea Salt & Crème Fraiche

Cheese Grits with Jalapeno

Coffee – Cranberry Juice – Orange Juice

BLACKBERRY MUFFINS WITH SUGARED PECAN TOPPING

Ingredients for Blackberry Muffins

- 1/4 lb.   Butter
- 1 cup   Sour Cream
- 1 tbls.   Buttermilk
- 3/4 cup   Sugar
- 2   Eggs
- 2 cups   Flour
- 1 tbls.   Baking Powder
- 1 1/2 cups Frozen Blackberries

Ingredients for Sugared Pecan Topping

- 1 cup   Sugar
- 1/2 cup   Flour
- 1/4 lb.   Butter
- 1 cup   Pecans

This is enough for two batches of Topping. I put leftover in a Ziploc bag and put in the freezer. It can go straight from the freezer on to the next batch of Muffins.

MAKES 1 DOZEN

1- In 2 qt. mixing bowl add Sour Cream, Buttermilk, Melted Butter, Sugar and Eggs. Stir with a wooden spoon until blended.

2- In a separate 3 qt. mixing bowl add Flour and Baking Powder, using wire whisk blend well.

3- Add the Sour Cream mixture to the Flour mixture. Mix with wooden spoon until you have a stiff batter.

4- Slowly add the frozen Blackberries. Do not over mix.

5- Spray Oil into a muffin tin that holds 12 muffins.

6- Evenly distribute the batter into the tins.

In a food processor

1- Add Sugar and Flour, pulse to blend.

2- Turn off processor and cut chilled Butter into 6 pieces and add to the mixture.

3- Pulse for a few seconds to break Butter up to smaller pieces.

4- Add Pecans and pulse for a few seconds more. Your mixture should be crumbly. Do not over process.

CRANBERRY ORANGE MUFFINS

MAKES 1 DOZEN

Use the same ingredients as the Blackberry but substitute Cranberries and add 3 tbls. of Grated Orange Peel

1- In 2 qt. mixing bowl add Sour Cream, Buttermilk, Melted Butter, Sugar and Eggs. Stir with a wooden spoon until blended.

2- In a separate 3 qt. mixing bowl add Flour and Baking Powder, using wire whisk blend well.

3- Add the Sour Cream mixture to the Flour mixture. Mix with wooden spoon until you have a stiff batter.

4- Slowly add Fresh Cranberries and Grated Orange Peel. Do not over mix.

5- Spray Oil into a muffin tin that holds 12 muffins.

6- Evenly distribute the batter into the tins.

Instead of adding the topping you can just sprinkle white sugar on top before baking.

CINNAMON ROLLS WITH CARAMEL GLAZE

MAKES 3 DOZEN

1- In Mixing bowl using a Dough Hook on your mixer add Yeast and Flour. Mix for 30 seconds.

2- In sauce pan slowly warm Milk, Butter, Sugar and Salt to 120 degrees.

3- With the mixer on low, add the warm Milk Mixture to dry mixture to activate Yeast.

4- Beat Eggs into the Dough one at time

5- Remove Dough and put in a large lightly oiled bowl. Set in warm place. Let rise for 1 hour or until dough has doubled in size.

6- Remove dough from bowl, divide into 3 balls. Each one should be rolled out on a lightly floured surface until dough is 21-inches long by 16-inches wide and 1/4-inch thick.

7- Blend Cinnamon Filling in food processor then spread on rolled Dough.

8- Roll dough from the top to bottom edge. Cut rolled dough into 1 3/4-inch slices and place on parchment paper while you prepare the pan.

Makes at least 3 dozen rolls - I freeze the unbaked rolls and let them thaw to room temperature and bake them. This works well.

9- About 8-9 Cinnamon Rolls fit in a 9 inch round cake pan.

10- First add 1/4 lb. Melted Butter with 1 1/2 cup of Brown Sugar to each 9 inch cake pan you are going to use. Pecans are optional. I prefer them.

11- Place Cinnamon Rolls in the pan and let rise for another 15 minutes.

12- Place in 350 degree oven and bake for 35 minutes.

13- Turn out on a serving platter. The Caramel Glaze should be on top of rolls. (Like a pineapple upside down cake).

Ingredients for Cinnamon Rolls

Dough for Cinnamon Rolls
- 4 packets   Active Dry Yeast
- 8 cups   All-Purpose Flour

Mix the two dry ingredients

- 2 cups   Milk
- 2 sticks   Butter
- 1 cup   Sugar
- ½ teas.   Salt

- 6   Eggs

Cinnamon Filling
- 1.5 cup   Brown Sugar firmly packed
- ½ cup   Flour
- 4.5 tbls.   Ground Cinnamon
- 1 cup   Butter

Blend in food processor

Caramel Glaze for bottom of Pan
- 1/4 stick   Melted Butter
- 1 1/2 cups   Brown Sugar Pecans are optional.

If you prefer a more traditional glaze-
Vanilla Glaze
- 1/2 cup   Butter, softened
- 1 1/2 cups   Sifted Powdered Sugar
- 1 (3-ounce)   Cream Cheese, softened
- 1/2 teas.   Vanilla extract
- 1/8 teas.   Salt

BROWN SUGAR SMOKED BACON ON SKEWERS

SERVES 12
Preheat oven to 375 degrees

1- Spray Wooden Skewers with Spray Oil.

2- Skewer Bacon with an up and down motion. You should have the Bacon skewered in a ribbon effect.

3- Place the Skewered Bacon on a baking rack that has been placed in a sheet pan.

4- Generously sprinkle Brown Sugar on each Skewer of Bacon.

5- Bake in 375 degree oven for approx. 30 minutes, until Bacon is cooked but not overly crisp.

Ingredients for Brown Sugar Smoked Bacon on Skewers		
•	24	Thick Slices of Smoked Bacon
•	2 cups	Brown Sugar
•	24	10 inch Wooden Skewers

SPIRAL SLICED HAM WITH POMEGRANATE AND PINEAPPLE GLAZE

Ingredients for Ham with Pomegranate and Pineapple		
•	1 cup	Crushed Pineapple
•	1 cup	Pomegranate Seeds
•	4 tbls.	Butter
•	1 cup	Brown Sugar
•	1/4 teas.	Ground Ginger

For a Spiral Sliced Ham with the bone still in estimate one pound per two guests for this Buffet Menu

MAKES 3 CUPS

1- In sauce pan melt Butter and Brown Sugar, adding Pineapple, Pomegranate Seeds and Ginger.

2- Cook for fifteen minutes until Syrup has thickened.

3- Pour one cup over Ham and bake at 375 degrees for 20 minutes to heat.

4- Save the other two cups to serve on the side with the Ham.

Scrambled Eggs with Smoked Sea salt and Crème Fraiche

SERVES 12

To make Crème Fraiche- mix 1 cup of Heavy Cream with a 1/4 cup of Buttermilk. Mix in a glass jar and cover. Set at room temperature (70 degrees) for 24 hours. Stir and refrigerate. This keeps refrigerated for 7 days.

1- Break 24 Eggs into a mixing bowl.

2- Add 1 teas. of Smoked Sea Salt, 1/4 cup of Heavy Whipping Cream, and a 1/2 cup of Crème Fraiche (save the other half for topping the Eggs and a half teaspoon of Smoked Sea Salt for topping the Crème Fraiche).

3- Mix with a wire whisk until the Eggs are well beaten

4- Slowly melt 3 tbls. Butter in a large non-stick sauté pan. This is for half the egg batter.

5- Use a rubber spatula and do not let Eggs brown. Pour into a bowl and set in warm place while you scramble the other half. Slightly under cook the Eggs if you are putting in a chafing dish.

6- Place in Chafing Dish and top with Crème Fraiche and Smoked Sea Salt.

Ingredients for Scrambled Eggs with Smoked Sea Salt		
•	24	Large Eggs
•	1/4 cup	Heavy Cream
•	1 1/2 teas.	Smoked Sea Salt
•	6 tbls.	Butter
Ingredients for Crème Fraiche		
•	1 cup	Heavy Cream
•	1/4 cup	Buttermilk

Cheese Grits with Jalapeno

MAKES 10 - 12 SERVINGS

1- Follow directions on box of Quaker Quick Grits to make six cups of cooked Grits.

2- In small sauce pan melt Butter, Cream Cheese and add Garlic.

3- In mixing bowl add Grits, while they are still warm, Butter and Cream Cheese mixture, Corn, Cheese, Jalapenos and Salt. Mix well.

Option - if you want this dish more "soufflé like" beat Eggs and Cream until pale yellow and fold into mixture. Increase baking time by 30 minutes.

4- Spray baking dish with spray Oil and then pour Grits into baking dish. Bake at 350 degrees for 20 minutes, or 50 minutes if you added Eggs and Cream.

Ingredients for Cheese Grits with Jalapeno		
•	6 cups	Cooked Grits
•	8 oz.	Cream Cheese
•	1/4 lb.	Butter
•	2 cups	Grated Sharp Cheddar Cheese
•	2 teas.	Roasted Garlic
•	1 cup	Cooked Yellow Corn
•	2 tbls.	Minced Pickled Jalapeno
•		Salt to taste (start with 1 teas. and adjust to taste)
Optional - 4 Eggs and 3/4 cup of Cream.		

BUTTER BISCUITS RECIPE ON PAGE 154
FIG PRESERVES RECIPE ON PAGE 116

Festive Brunch

Menu

Spiked Apple Cider

Popover Pancakes with Raspberry Jam

Sausage and Creole Cream Cheese Bread

Sautéed Bananas

Savory Grits with
Shrimp & Andouille Creole

Cranberry Gingerbread Cake
with Cinnamon Whipped Cream

SAUSAGE & CREOLE CREAM CHEESE BREADS

MAKES 2 LOAVES OF BREAD
Fill one with Sausage & Mozzarella and the other with Creole Cream Cheese filling.

1- Combine Milk, Water and Margarine in sauce pan. Heat over low heat until mixture is warm (120 degrees). Margarine does not need to melt all the way.

2- Put 3 1/2 cups Flour, Sugar, Salt and Yeast in mixing bowl. Use dough hook on mixer. Turn to low speed and mix 15 seconds.

3- Gradually add warm Milk mixture while mixing for another minute.

4- Continue on low speed, add remaining Flour a half cup at a time, until Dough clings to the dough hook and cleans sides of bowl. This should be about 2 minutes. Place in Oiled metal, glass or wooden bowl to let rise for one hour.

5- While Dough is rising make fillings.

Italian Sausage filling- In sauté pan, brown Italian Sausage. Drain all excess grease. Put in a bowl to cool. Put one cup of grated Mozzarella in a separate bowl.
Cream Cheese filling- In food processor blend Cream Cheese, Cottage Cheese, Egg and Sugar for a few seconds until smooth.

6- Turn Dough onto Floured cloth or board. Cut into 2 equal pieces. Roll out into rectangles 10x14 inches.

7- Fill one rectangle with Italian Sausage and Mozzarella. Roll and tuck edges under. Fill the second rectangle with the Cream Cheese filling. Spread evenly, roll and tuck the edges under.

8- Mix Egg and Water together to make Egg Wash. Brush tops with Egg Wash.

9- Preheat oven to 375 degrees. Place Dough on lightly Oiled baking sheets. The loaves cook better on separate sheets.

10- Bake for one hour. You can test by thumping the loaf. It should have a hollow sound.

11- Let cool for 10 minutes.

12- Cut off the ends and slice into 1 inch slices. Serve warm.

Ingredients for Two Loaves of Bread

- 1 cup   Milk
- 1/2 cup   Water
- 1/4 cup   Margarine
- 4-5 cups   All Purpose Flour
- 1 tbls.   Sugar
- 1 teas.   Salt
- 2 packages   Dry Active Yeast

Ingredients for Sausage Filling

- 1 lb.   Ground Hot Italian Sausage
- 1 cup   Grated Mozzarella

Ingredients for Cream Cheese Filling

- 8 oz.   Cream Cheese
- 4 oz.   Small Curd Cottage Cheese
- 1   Egg
- 1/4 cup   Sugar

Egg Wash for top of Bread

- 1   Egg
- 1/2 cup   Water

Letting Dough Rise-
The ideal temperature for Dough to rise is 85 degrees. The top of the refrigerator is often a warm place. I find my Dough rises best when I'm cooking a lot of other things. Since that is not always the case...you can use the old method of setting your bowl over a pot of 90 degree water. As the water cools down, empty some and add some more hot tap water. Use your thermometer to check the temperature of the water.

POPOVER PANCAKES

MAKES 12 MUFFIN SIZE OR 2 EIGHT INCH PAN SIZE

1- In blender add Eggs and Powdered Sugar then whip for 1 minute.

2- Melt Butter then add Milk, heat to warm.

3- Add Butter and Milk mixture to Egg mixture and blend for a few seconds.

4- Gradually add the Flour until you have a smooth Batter.

5- Preheat oven to 425 degrees. Then Oil and heat muffin tins.

6- Pour Batter into hot pans, fill half way and bake at 425 degrees for 20-25 minutes. Do not open the oven while baking or the Cakes will fall.

7- Sprinkle Powdered Sugar on top.

Serve right away, although they will hold their shape and still taste good for over an hour. You can reheat just before serving if needed.

Ingredients for Popover Pancakes		
•	4	Eggs
•	1/4 cup	Powdered Sugar
•	1 1/2 cups	Warm Milk
•	1/2 cup	Melted Butter
•	1 cup	Flour
•	3 tbls.	Powdered Sugar
•		Spray Oil

RASPBERRY JAM

MAKES 2 PINTS
Use a candy thermometer to check temperatures

1- In sauce pan that has a thick bottom add Sugar, Orange Peel and Orange Juice.

2- Cook over medium heat until the Sugar is at least 220 degrees.

3- Add Raspberries and continue to cook until this thickens. Bring to about 300 degrees.

Refrigerate if you don't heat process in canning jars. This may be frozen if you won't be using it within three or four days.

Ingredients for Raspberry Jam		
•	3 cups	Raspberries (frozen are fine)
•	2 1/2 cups	Sugar
•	2 teas.	Grated Orange Peel
•	3 tbls.	Orange Juice
•	Optional	1/4 cup of Golden Raisins

RECIPE FOR SAUTÉED BANANAS ON PAGE 22

SHRIMP-ANDOUILLE CREOLE

MAKES 8 SERVINGS
To make Dark Roux - in heavy iron skillet brown equal amounts of Oil and Flour and stir until chocolate brown.
You can purchase premade Roux from the market and it is very good.

1- In large sauce pan, brown diced Andouille, add Onion and Bell Pepper and sauté for 2 minutes.

2- Add Green Onions, Garlic and Basil. Cook for another minute.

3- Add Diced Tomatoes in Juice, Tomato Puree.

4- In separate pan dissolve Roux with 1 cup of water and add to the Creole Sauce.

5- Cut the Lemon into four thick round slices and add to the Creole Sauce.

6- Add 1/2 tbls. of Cajun Seasoning Salt to start. You will have to add to taste because all the brands have a different Salt content.
Just season and taste as you go.

7- Let the Sauce simmer for 30-40 minutes. You will add the Shrimp just before serving.

The Lemon may be removed or left for garnish. It is not really an edible part of this dish but it is essential to the flavor.

This will be served over Savory Grits.

Ingredients for Andouille-Shrimp Creole

•	1 lbs	Diced Andouille
•	2 cups	Diced Onion
•	1 1/2 cup	Diced Bell Pepper
•	1/2 cup	Diced Green Onion
•	2 tbls.	Minced Garlic
•	2 tbls.	Minced Fresh Basil
•	3 cups	Diced Tomatoes in Juice
•	1 cup	Tomato Puree
•	1 cup	Water
•	1/2 cup	Dark Roux
•	1	Lemon
•	1 tbls.	Cajun Seasoning Salt
•	3 lbs.	Shrimp peeled and deveined

SAVORY GRITS

Ingredients for Savory Grits

•	6 cups	Cooked Grits
•	8 oz.	Cream Cheese
•	1/4 lb.	Butter
•	2 cups	Grated Mozzarella
•	2 teas.	Roasted Garlic
•	2 tbls.	Rosemary
•	2 teas.	Thyme

Salt to taste

(start with 1 teas. of salt and adjust to taste)

Optional - 4 Eggs and 3/4 cup of Cream.

MAKES 10 TO 12 SERVINGS

1- Follow directions on box of Quaker Quick Grits to make six cups of cooked Grits.
2- In small sauce pan melt Butter, Cream Cheese and add Garlic.
3- In mixing bowl add Grits, while they are still warm, Butter and Cream Cheese mixture, Mozzarella Cheese, Herbs and Salt. Mix well.
Option - if you want this dish more "soufflé like" beat Eggs and Cream until pale yellow and fold into mixture. Increase baking time by 30 minutes.
4- Spray baking dish with spray Oil and then pour Grits into baking dish. Bake at 350 degrees for 20 minutes, or 50 minutes if you added Eggs and Cream.

CRANBERRY GINGERBREAD CAKE

MAKES 10 SERVINGS
You will need an oblong cake pan or 9x13 baking dish. Spray well with Oil.

1- Sift all dry ingredients together.

2- Cream Margarine and Sugar together until fluffy. Then add Egg until blended in well, add Molasses and Buttermilk.

3- Gradually sift in Flour mixture until blended.

4- Fold in Cranberries.

5- Pour into well greased pan.

6- Bake at 350 degrees for 50 minutes or until center is done.

Variations- Peaches and Blackberries are good in this when they are in season.

Ingredients for Cranberry Gingerbread Cake

- 2 cups — Flour
- 2 teas. — Baking Powder
- 1/4 teas. — Baking Soda
- 1/2 teas. — Salt
- 1 1/2 teas. — Ginger
- 1 teas. — Cinnamon
- 1/2 cup — Margarine
- 1 cup — Sugar
- 1 — Egg
- 2/3 cup — Molasses
- 3/4 cup — Buttermilk
- 1 cup — Cranberries

Ingredients for Cinnamon Whipped Cream

- 2 pints — Whipping Cream
- 1 cup — Sugar
- 1 teas. — Cinnamon

CINNAMON WHIPPED CREAM

MAKES 1 1/2 QUARTS

1- In chilled mixing bowl pour in cold Whipping Cream, with electric mixer on the low speed whip until very soft peaks begin to form.

2- Keeping mixer on low speed gradually add Sugar and Cinnamon. You want peaks to form but you don't want the Cream too stiff.

3- Keep refrigerated until ready to use.

SPIKED APPLE CIDER

Makes 24 Servings

1- In large pot heat Apple Cider, Cinnamon and Nutmeg. Do not boil, just keep at a simmer. Add Tuaca and Dark Rum before serving.

Whipped Cream with Cinnamon Sugar may be used to create a drink called Hot Apple Pie. For this recipe I add more Tuaca and less Rum.

Ingredients for Spiked Apple Cider

- 1 gal. — Apple Cider
- 1/2 teas. — Cinnamon
- 1/4 teas. — Nutmeg
- 1/2 cup — Tuaca
- 1 cup — Dark Rum

Roast Lobster
in the Fireplace

Menu

Asparagus   Red Potatoes
Roasted Peppers
Asiago & Croton Poivre
Cheeses

Roast Lobster
flavored with Garlic & Basil

Lemon-Caper Mayonnaise

XXX Smores
with Tia Maria Soaked
Marshmallows
& Dark Sweet Chocolate

WINTER COLD PLATE

MAKES 4 SERVINGS
Arrange on a decorative serving plate.

1- Roast Asparagus (recipe on page 173).

2- Cut small Red New Potatoes in half. Cover with cold water and bring to a boil. Cook for another 10-12 minutes. The Potatoes should be cooked all the way through but still firm enough to hold their shape. Cool and add to plate.

3- Preheat oven to 400 degrees. Place Red Bell Peppers on baking sheet and roast until the skin is blistered. Cool and cut Pepper into strips, removing the seeds. Arrange on plate.

4- Arrange Cheeses on plate. Keep plate chilled until ready to serve.

5- Heat Bread and serve with Cold Plate.

Ingredients for Winter Cold Plate		
•	1 lb.	Roast Asparagus
•	12	Small New Red Potatoes
•	2	Sweet Red Bell Peppers
•	4 oz.	Asiago Cheese
•	4 oz.	Croton Poivre Cheese
•	1 loaf	Country Style Italian or French Bread

You may substitute any of your favorite firmer cheeses.

Ingredients for Lemon Caper Mayonnaise		
•	2	Egg Yolks
•	Dash	Salt and White Pepper
•	2 tbls.	Lemon Juice
•	1 tbls.	Dijon Mustard
•	1 1/4 cup	Salad Oil
•	2 tbls.	Capers

LEMON CAPER MAYONNAISE

MAKES 2 CUPS

1- In food processor whip Egg Yolks with a dash of Salt and White Pepper. Add Lemon Juice and continue to whip until Yolks are creamy lemon yellow.

2- Add Mustard and continue to beat. Slowly add Oil to make a creamy Mayonnaise.

3- Add Capers and pulse once.

Chill and serve with Roasted Lobster and Cold Plate.

ROAST LOBSTER IN THE FIREPLACE

MAKES 4 SERVINGS
For this dish I prefer the Warm Water Lobster tails. The frozen ones are fine for this dish.
You can do these on the grill or in the oven if you don't have a fireplace. Even if you don't have a fireplace you should serve this meal on the floor, picnic style. It is refreshing to do this in the middle of Winter.

1- Split each Lobster down the back of the shell with a knife.
I place the Lobster on a cutting board, then place the knife in the center of the back and take a hammer to hit the knife down. I find this safe and easy.

2- Melt the Butter and add Garlic, Basil, Lemon Juice and Worcestershire.

3- Season the Lobsters well with Salt and Pepper then put them meat side down into the Butter mixture for at least one hour before roasting.

4- Using Campfire sticks (that are used for roasting Hot Dogs) put Lobster on securely, just as you would a Hot Dog.

5- Roast over open fire for 12-20 minutes. The Meat will become more white and not opaque. Don't put too close to the flames or it will char.

Ingredients for Roast Lobster in the Fireplace

•	4	8 oz. Warm Water Lobster Tails in the Shell
•	1/4 lb.	Butter
•	2 tbls.	Minced Garlic
•	2 tbls.	Minced Basil
•	2 teas.	Fresh Lemon Juice
•	2 teas.	Worcestershire Sauce
•	1/4 teas.	Salt
•	1/4 teas.	Black Pepper

XXX SMORES

MAKES 4 SERVINGS

1- Tear off four pieces of aluminum foil 12x8 inches.

2- Place Marshmallows in bowl and pour Tia Maria Liqueur over them. Toss to distribute Liqueur evenly.

3- Place 1 Graham Cracker on each piece of foil, add 4 oz. of Chocolate on top of Cracker then three Marshmallows on top of Chocolate.

4- Top with another Graham Cracker and wrap in the foil. Wrap by folding, it is easier to undo when you are ready to serve.

5- Using long tongs, place in fireplace for just 3-5 minutes and serve.

Ingredients for XXX Smores

•	8	Graham Crackers
•	12	Large Marshmallows
•	1/2 cup	Tia Maria Liqueur
•	2	8 oz. bars of Dark Sweet Chocolate

Preferably Valrhona or any good brand of Chocolate that you can find.

Pecans are a nice addition if you like.

Italian Cooking Class
at Twin Oaks

Menu

Porcini Custard with White Shrimp
on a bed of Smoked Bacon & Spinach with Lemon

Caesar Salad
with White Truffle Toast

Timpano
Pastry filled with penne pasta, tomato ragout, meatballs,
poached chicken, boiled egg and peas

Pineapple Short Cake with Crème Brule Ice Cream

PORCINI CUSTARD WITH WHITE SHRIMP

MAKES 10-12 SERVINGS

You will need custard cups sprayed with Pam or a cooking oil. Place oiled custard cups in a baking pan with 1 inch of water in the bottom of the baking pan. Preheat oven to 350 degrees.

1- In sauté Pan melt 1 tbls. Butter and sauté Sliced Baby Porcini Mushrooms. Add fresh Ground Pepper. You do not need Salt because the Bouillon is salty. Let cool.

2- In 2 qt. mixing bowl beat Egg Yolks with whisk for about 30 seconds then add Cream.

3- Dissolve the one Bouillon cube in 1/4 cup of boiling water. Let cool down for ten minutes before whisking into Egg Yolk and Cream mixture.

4- Add Mushrooms and stir.

5- Fill Custard cups with 5-6 oz. of mixture. Stir frequently to keep Mushrooms well distributed.

6- Bake at 350 degrees for 50-60 minutes until set.

7- When ready to serve sauté Shrimp with Butter, Minced Garlic, Italian herbs and finish with Fresh Basil.

8- Place sautéed Spinach on plate, then turn the Custard out of the glass cups onto the plate and top with sautéed Shrimp.

If you can find it my favorite brand of Porcini Bouillon cubes is Star. There are many on the market and there is Mushroom Bouillon available. I find it in many groceries in major cities. If you can not find it you may substitute a Vegetarian Bouillon Cube or Chicken.

Ingredients for Porcini Custard		
•	1 lb.	Sliced Baby Porcinis
•	1 tbls.	Butter
•	1 teas.	Minced Garlic
•	1/2 teas.	Fresh Ground Pepper
•	9 each	Egg Yolks
•	2 1/2 cups	Heavy Cream
•	1	Porcini Bouillon Cube diluted in 1/4 cup boiling water
•	3 tbls.	Butter
•	1/2 teas.	Minced Garlic
•	1 teas.	Mixed Italian Herbs
•	36	Medium White Shrimp (peeled and deveined)
•	2 teas.	Fresh Basil (minced)

Ingredients		
•	4	Strips of Smoked Bacon diced
•	1 lb.	Baby Spinach Leaves
Juice of half a lemon		
•	Salt- optional	
•	Anchovy- optional	

SPINACH WITH BACON AND LEMON

MAKES 6 SERVINGS

1- Dice Smoked Bacon and cook until crisp. Remove half the Bacon fat.

2- Add the Spinach stirring until it is slightly wilted and add Lemon Juice.

3- Serve immediately.
I like Anchovy with this dish, but I have to say Anchovy is not to everyone's taste. It is optional. Adding Salt is rarely needed because of the Salt in Smoked Bacon.

CAESAR SALAD WITH WHITE TRUFFLE TOASTS

To Make Dressing-
In Blender
1- Add Anchovy Filets, Garlic Cloves and Egg Yolks and puree for 30 seconds.
2- Add Lemon Juice and Red Wine Vinegar and blend for 15 seconds.
3- Add Worcestershire Sauce and Dijon Mustard and blend for another 30 seconds.
4- Slowly add Olive Oil through the hole in the top of the blender while it is blending (you want your dressing to be thick and creamy).
5- Add the Parmesan Cheese and blend for 15 seconds.

To Make White Truffle Butter
Soften Butter and using whisk, slowly whip with 2 tbls. of White Truffle Oil. Keep at room temperature and spread generously on top of toasted French Bread Rounds to serve with Salad.

To Put Salad together
1- Take Crisp, clean Romaine Hearts and cut Length-wise (from top to bottom) first in half and half again. You should have long 1/2 inch strips of Romaine. Depending on the size of Romaine you may need to cut again. The presentation is better than using chopped Romaine.
2- In bowl add desired amount of Dressing to Romaine and gently toss to cover with Dressing. Toss by hand several times gently enough to cover with Dressing but leaving the leaves pointing in the same direction.
3- Place Lettuce Leaves on salad plate and garnish with grated Parmesan.
4- Place two White Truffle Butter Toast on each plate and serve.

Ingredients for Caesar Dressing

•	8	Anchovy Filets
•	2	Garlic Cloves
•	2	Egg Yolks
•	1 tbls.	Lemon Juice
•	1 tbls.	Red Wine Vinegar
•	1/2 teas.	Worcestershire Sauce
•	1 tbls.	Dijon Mustard
•	1 cup	Olive Oil
•	1/2 cup	Parmesan Cheese

This makes two cups of dressing so you have more for later. It keeps 5-6 days in the refrigerator if covered well.

Ingredients for Salad for 6

•	3	Crisp Romaine Hearts (cold)
•	12	Toasted French Bread Rounds use small baguette.
•	1 cup	Caesar Dressing
•	1/2 cup	Grated Parmesan Cheese

Ingredients for White Truffle Butter

•	1/4 lb.	Soft Salted Butter
•	2 tbls.	White Truffle Oil

Ingredient List for Timpano

This is your shopping list and get organized list.

Ingredients for Pastry

5 lbs.	Flour
3/4 lb.	Butter
2 lb.	Margarine
2	Egg yolks
*ice cold water	

Ingredients for Ragout

2	Medium Onions
2	Celery Ribs
2	Carrots
1/2 cup	Flat Leaf Italian Parsley
12	Cloves of Garlic
4 oz.	Pancetta (or Smoked Bacon)
2 lbs.	Pork Ribs
1 bottle	Red Wine
8 oz.	Tomato Paste
2/ 60 oz. cans	Italian Plum Tomatoes
8	Fennel Sausages
1 tbls.	Ground Oregano
1 tbls.	Crushed Red Pepper
2 tbls.	Fresh Minced Basil
2 teas.	Salt
2 teas.	Black Pepper

Ingredients for Meatballs

1 lb.	Ground Beef
1 lb.	Ground Pork
1 cup	Diced, Sautéed Onion
1 tbls.	Fresh Minced Basil
2 tbls.	Fresh Minced Garlic
1 teas.	Ground Oregano
3	Eggs
1 1/2 cups	Bread Crumbs
1 teas.	Salt
1 teas.	Crushed Red Pepper

Ingredients for Poached Chicken Breasts

3	Boneless Chicken Breasts
3	Shallots
1 cup	White Wine
1 teas.	Salt
1 teas.	Pepper

Other Ingredients

4 cups	Cooked Penne Pasta
2 cups	Green Peas
5	Boiled Eggs
2 cups	Grated Parmesan Cheese
3 cups	Grated Mozzarella

PASTRY FOR TIMPANO

Refer to ingredient list

*ice cold water is best for pastry.

Directions:

1- In large metal bowl, add Flour and Salt.

2- Cut Butter & Margarine into small cubes.

3- Add Butter and Margarine to Flour and work in with fingers until the size of peas.

4- Beat Egg Yolk and mix in.

5- Add just enough cold Water to bring the Dough together.

6- Press into 4 equal size balls and refrigerate.

7- Chill for at least two hours or overnight.

8- Spray a gallon size metal bowl with spray Oil.

9- Roll out dough and line the bowl with it. Take the rest of the dough and roll out a round to cover the top of the Timpano once it is filled. Use the opening of the bowl to measure how large of a top you need.

Ingredients for Savory Ragout		
•	2	Medium Onions
•	2	Celery Ribs
•	2	Carrots
•	1/2 cup	Flat Leaf Italian Parsley
•	12	Cloves of Garlic
•	4 oz.	Pancetta (or Smoked Bacon)
•	2 lbs.	Pork Ribs
•	1 bottle	Red Wine
•	8 oz.	Tomato paste
•	2	60 oz. cans Italian Plum Tomatoes
•	8	Fennel Sausages
•	1 tbls.	Ground Oregano
•	1 tbls.	Crushed Red Pepper
•	2 tbls.	Fresh Minced Basil
•	2 teas.	Salt
•	2 teas.	Black Pepper

Directions for Ragout

1- In food processor chop Onion, Celery and Carrots. Use the pulse button. You <u>do not</u> want to puree the Vegetables. You want them to be coarse.

2- In large heavy sauce pot, brown Pancetta, Pork Ribs and Fennel Sausages. Turn and make sure they are well browned.

3- Add the chopped Onions, Celery and Carrots, stir and cook for 5 minutes.

4- Chop the Garlic and Flat Leaf Parsley and add to pot.

5- Add the bottle of Red Wine and scrape the bottom of the pot.

6- Add Tomato Paste and Plum Tomatoes.

7- Simmer for one hour.

8- Remove and save the Fennel Sausage (it will be put into the Timpano).

9- Add Oregano, Crushed Red Pepper, Basil, Salt and Black Pepper.

10- Continue to simmer for one hour more.

11- Take the Ribs out, they are not used in the Timpano but are wonderful with sauce & pasta.

Recipe for Meatballs and Poached Chicken for Timpano

Meatballs for Timpano

1 lb.	Ground Beef
1 lb.	Ground Pork
1 cup	Diced, Sautéed Onion
1 tbls.	Fresh Minced Basil
2 tbls.	Fresh Minced Garlic
1 teas.	Ground Oregano
3	Eggs
1 1/2 cups	Bread Crumbs
1 teas.	Salt
1 teas.	Crushed Red Pepper

Directions-

1- In large mixing bowl add Beef, Pork and Sautéed Onion, Basil, Garlic, Oregano, Eggs, Bread Crumbs, Salt and Crushed Red Pepper.

2- Mix and knead until well blended.

3- Using Tablespoon, portion and roll to round Meatballs (the size of a quarter). You should have approximately 36 small Meatballs.

4- Place on baking sheet and brown in 350 degree oven. Do not over cook because they will cook more in the Timpano.

Poached Chicken Breasts

3	Boneless Chicken Breasts
3	Shallots
1 cup	White wine
1 cup	Water
1 teas.	Salt
1 teas.	Pepper

Directions-

1- In deep sauté pan add Shallots, White Wine, Water, Salt and Pepper.

2- Bring to a simmer and cook for 10 minutes.

3- Add skinless, boneless Chicken Breasts and poach for 12-14 minutes.

4- Cool, then slice at an angle.

Other Ingredients for Timpano

4 cups	Cooked Penne Pasta
2 cups	Green Peas
5	Peeled Boiled Eggs
2 cups	Grated Parmesan Cheese
3 cups	Grated Mozzarella

THE FINAL ASSEMBLY

PUTTING TIMPANO TOGETHER

1- After lining bowl with Pastry place a layer of Meatballs.

2- Add a little Ragout and sprinkle Grated Mozzarella.

3- Layer Green Peas.

4- Sprinkle Grated Parmesan and Sliced Poached Chicken Breasts.

5- Layer quartered Boiled Eggs.

6- Layer sliced Fennel Sausage.

7- Add a little Ragout and sprinkle Grated Mozzarella.

8- Mix 4 cups of cooked Penne Pasta with 4 cups of Ragout, add as another layer.

9- Add more Parmesan.

10-Add more Meatballs and Sausage and Ragout.

11- Place Pastry Crust on top. Pinch sides to seal Timpano. Pierce several holes with a fork to let steam out while cooking.

12- Cook in 325 degree oven for 2 hours. To test, tap on the top and Pastry should be firm and when you tap it should sound hollow. (Like a sound of a drum or Timpano).

13- Let Timpano rest for at least 15–20 minutes.

14- Cover top with a serving tray, then carefully turn over.

15- Bring to the table and let everyone tap on it with their forks. This will help loosen the Pastry.

16- Then lift the bowl. It should be brown and beautiful.

17- Slice and serve.

18- If you have left over Ragout, it is nice to have it on the table to serve with the Timpano. If there is no Ragout left over, then you have enough in the Timpano already.

CRÈME BRULEE ICE CREAM

Ingredients for Crème Brulee Ice Cream

- 2 cups — Sugar
- 1 pint — Heavy Cream
- 8 — Egg Yolks
- 1 1/2 cups — Half & Half
- 2 tbls. — Vanilla Extract

The Ice Cream and Topping are so good that I do not spend so much time on the short cake.
I often use pre-made short cakes from the grocery. Or I bake a sheet cake and cut into 3 inch rounds.
You can also purchase a Pound Cake or use Sweet Biscuits as a short cake.

PINEAPPLE SAUCE FOR SHORT CAKE

MAKES 8 SERVINGS

1- In large sauté pan, over medium heat, melt Butter, then add Brown Sugar.

2- Add Lemon Juice, Orange Juice and Orange Zest (if you don't have a zester you can finely grate the Orange Peel). Continue to cook until Brown Sugar has cooked to a Syrup.

3- Peel Pineapple, core Pineapple then cut length-wise, then in thirds. You want the pieces to be about two inches each. Add Pineapple to Brown Sugar Syrup in the pan.

4- Add the Rum and Cinnamon. Heat for just about 2 minutes You want the Pineapple to remain firm.

5- Spoon warm Pineapple in Rum flavored Syrup over Short Cake. Then top with Crème Brulee Ice Cream.

MAKES 1 QUART
The better quality your Vanilla, the better your Ice Cream.

1- Put Sugar into heavy skillet and caramelize. Use a heavy duty pot holder to hold the handle of the skillet so you do not burn yourself. Tilt the skillet to evenly brown the Sugar. When the Sugar is dark brown, but not burned, immediately add the Cream. This will stop the Sugar from burning. Cook until all the Sugar has dissolved.
2- Beat the Egg Yolk with the Half & Half and Vanilla.
3- Place the Egg mixture over a double boiler and begin to heat. Slowly add in the Sugar & Cream mixture. Stir with a wire whisk.
4- Cook your Custard mixture over medium heat for about 12 minutes until it will coat a wooden spoon.
5- Pour into another bowl and refrigerate. The Custard should be completely cooled before you put it into the ice cream freezer.

I would make the Ice Cream very early in the day or, even better, the day before your party.
Helpful Notes-
Too much Water or Alcohol will make Ice Cream granular. Too little Sugar or Fat (from the Milk) will also make the Ice Cream granular.

Be sure your Ice Cream churn scrapes the sides well.

Do not freeze too fast.

Ingredients for Pineapple Topping

- 1 — Fresh Pineapple
- 1/4 lb. — Butter
- 2 cup — Brown Sugar
- 1 teas. — Fresh Lemon Juice
- 1 tbls. — Fresh Orange Juice
- 1 teas. — Orange Zest
- 3 tbls. — Dark Rum
- 1/4 teas. — Cinnamon

Holiday Cocktail Party
Menu

Mistletoe Martinis and Natchez Eggnog

Andouille-Crawfish Cheese Cake

Stuffed Loin of Pork
in Ginger, Orange, Black pepper Glaze

Cheddar Biscuits   Rosemary Rolls
Ginger Honey Mustard

Pickled Shrimp

Oysters & Mushrooms on Garlic Toasts

Caramelized Onion and Tomato Pastries

Jalapeno Corn Muffins with
Smoked Chicken Salad

Bourbon-Pecan Truffles

MISTLETOE MARTINI

The key to a perfect Martini is to make it "black & blue". You take two long spoons and you hit the ice hard as you are mixing. This makes the drink colder and retains little ice shavings when you strain and pour. The perfect Martini, in my book, has ice crystals floating on top.

You need a Martini Pitcher (makes 4-5 at a time).

1- Fill pitcher with ice, pour in 3/4 cup of Vodka, close to 1&1/2 oz. per drink.

2- Add 3 teas. of Grenadine (Grenadine is a syrup made from Pomegranate). Add Juice from half a Lime.

3- Chill Martini glasses.

4- In each glass put three Pomegranate Seeds and a Mint Leaf for garnish. Use a strainer and pour a Martini in each glass.

Ingredients for Mistletoe Martini		
•	1 btl.	Stoli or Skyy Vodka
•	1 btl.	Grenadine
•		Seeds from a Pomegranate
•	4	Limes
Mint leaves for garnish		

NATCHEZ EGGNOG

MAKES 12-16 SERVINGS

1- Separate Eggs. In one bowl put Yolks and add Sugar, beat with electric mixer until the Yolks are very thick and creamy yellow, at least 5-7 minutes. Set aside.

2- In another bowl save only 8 of the 12 Whites (throw away four whites). Whip the Egg Whites until stiff peaks form. Stiff but not dry. Set aside.

3- Whip Cream until it forms soft peaks. Set aside.

4- In large container combine Half & Half, Cinnamon, Nutmeg, Vanilla, Rum and Bourbon. Stir in Egg Yolk mixture. Continue to stir until well blended.

5- With wire whisk, blend in Egg Whites and Whipped Cream.

6- Chill, then pour into punch bowl and serve.

Ingredients for Natchez Eggnog		
•	1 doz.	Pasteurized Eggs
•	2 cups	Sugar
•	1 pt.	Cream
•	2 qts.	Half & Half
•	1/2 teas.	Cinnamon
•	1 teas.	Nutmeg
•	1 teas.	Vanilla
•	1 cup	Rum
•	1 1/2 cups	Bourbon

ANDOUILLE-CRAWFISH CHEESE CAKE

MAKES 30 SERVINGS FOR A COCKTAIL PARTY

12 SERVINGS IF USED AS A FIRST COURSE OF A SEATED DINNER

1- Use a 9 inch Spring form Pan, spray well with spray oil.

2- In mixing bowl, mix Panko Bread Crumbs, Parmesan Cheese, Cajun Seasoning and Melted Butter.

3- Pat Crust Mixture into bottom and 1/2 inch up the sides.

4- Dice Andouille in 1/8 inch pieces. Saute Andouille add Oil, Onions, Peppers, Garlic and Spices. Drain extra liquid from Crawfish, dice Crawfish but not too small and add to Andouille. Set aside until you have the Cream Cheese Mixture prepared.

5- In Kitchen aid- Mix Softened Cream Cheese, Smoked Gouda, Cream and beat with paddle until smooth. Do not over mix. **Also note– Cream Cheese must be softened before this process begins or it will remain lumpy. Add the Eggs one at a time.

6- Add the Crawfish &Andouille and mix a few turns then add the Eggs last.

7- Pour over crust into Springform pan.

8- Preheat oven to 325°F. In a baking pan large enough to accommodate your Springform pan, add an inch or so of water to make a water bath.

9- Cut a piece of foil large enough to go around pan and wrap pan so no water can leak into it. Place Cheese Cake pan into a water bath in a baking pan. Bake for 1 1/2 hours or until set.

Let cool at least two hours - ideally 4 hour before cutting into portions- serve with warm Smoked Tomato Coulis Recipe on page 101 and Toasted French Bread.

Ingredients for Andouille-Crawfish Cheese Cake		
FOR THE CRUST		
•	1 cup	Panko Bread Crumbs
•	1 cup	Coarsely Grated Parmesan Cheese
•	1/2 teas.	Cajun Seasoning
•	1/2 cup	Melted Butter
•		
FOR THE FILLING		
•	1 lb.	Diced Andouille
•	1 tbls.	Olive Oil
•	1 cup	Minced Onion
•	1 cup	Minced Red & Green Bell Peppers
•	1 tbls.	Minced Garlic
•	1 teas.	Cajun seasoning
•	2 teas.	Cracked Black Pepper
•	1 lb.	Crawfish tail meat
•	1 1/2 lb.	Cream Cheese (softened)
•	1 1/2 cups	Grated Smoked Gouda Cheese
•	1/2 cup	Heavy Cream
•	4	Eggs (beaten)
•	1 teas.	Salt

GINGER, ORANGE & BLACK PEPPER GLAZE

MAKES 1 CUP

1- In small sauce pan melt Butter. Add Ginger, Orange, Garlic and Black Pepper. Cook over medium heat for one minute, then add Salt and Molasses.

2- Cool and use as marinade for Pork.

Ingredients for Ginger, Orange and Black Pepper Glaze	
• 1/4 lb.	Butter
• 2 tbls.	Minced Ginger
• 2 tbls.	Grated Orange Rind
• 2 tbls.	Minced Garlic
• 2 tbls.	Cracked Black Pepper
• 2 tbls.	Sea Salt
• 2 tbls.	Molasses

Ingredients for Stuffed Loin of Pork	
• 6 lbs.	Boneless Pork Loin
• 1 lb.	Andouille Sausage
• 1 cup	Ginger-Orange & Black Pepper Glaze
• 1/2 cup	Water

STUFFED LOIN OF PORK

MAKES 12 SERVINGS

1- When you purchase your Pork Loin, ask the Butcher to cut a hole in the center so you can stuff it with cooked links of Andouille Sausage.

2- Cook the Andouille Sausage links and slide into the Pork Loin.
When you go to slice the Pork it makes a nice presentation, the white Pork wrapped around the dark red Andouille.

3- Pour Glaze over Pork Loin at least one hour before cooking.

4- Bake at 350 degrees for 30 minutes. Add half cup of Water and cover and cook for another 30 to 40 minutes.

This should be cooked to about 140 degrees.

Let rest for 15 minutes before slicing.

For a Cocktail Party this should be presliced.

Side Note
The Pork Loin makes a great entrée for a dinner party.

You can serve it with the Roasted Garlic-Mustard Mashed Potatoes (recipe on page 170) or Baked Yams.

You can top the Baked Yam with Sour Cream and the Cranberry-Mango Chutney (recipe on page 172).

ROSEMARY ROLLS

MAKES 2 DOZEN ROLLS
This recipe makes a soft roll for sandwiches.

1- Combine Milk, Water and Margarine in sauce pan. Heat over low heat until mixture is warm (120 degrees). Margarine does not need to melt all the way.

2- Put 3 1/2 cups Flour, Sugar, Salt, Yeast and Rosemary in mixing bowl. Use dough hook on mixer. Turn to speed 2 and mix 15 seconds.

3- Gradually add warm Milk mixture while mixing for another minute.

4- Continue on speed 2, add remaining Flour a half cup at a time, until Dough clings to the dough hook and cleans sides of bowl. This should be about 2 minutes.

5- Turn Dough onto floured cloth or board. Cut into 24 equal pieces. Shape into Rolls.

6- Mix Egg and Water together to make Egg Wash. Brush tops with Egg Wash. Add a little chopped Rosemary and Sea Salt to top of each Roll.

7- Place on Oiled baking sheet and let rise in 90 degree oven for 15 minutes.

8- Turn oven up to 400 degrees and bake for 15 minutes or until golden brown.

Ingredients for Rosemary Rolls

- 1 cup — Milk
- 1/2 cup — Water
- 1/4 cup — Margarine
- 4-5 cups — All Purpose Flour
- 1 tbls. — Sugar
- 1 teas. — Salt
- 1 tbls. — Fresh Rosemary
- 2 packages — Dry Active Yeast

Ingredients for Egg Wash for top of Rolls

- 1 — Egg
- 1/2 cup — Water
- 2 tbls. — Fresh Rosemary
- 1 teas. — Sea Salt

GINGER-HONEY MUSTARD

MAKES 1 CUP

1- In food processor or blender add Ginger, Dry Mustard and Water, blend for a few seconds and let sit for ten minutes.

2- Add Honey and blend until smooth.

Ingredients for Ginger-Honey Mustard

- 2 tbls. — Candied Ginger
- 2 tbls. — Dry Mustard
- 1/4 cup — Water
- 1/2 cup — Honey

Oysters & Mushrooms

MAKES 24 SERVINGS

1- In large sauté pan add 2 tbls. of Butter, sauté Shallots and Garlic, then add Mushrooms and cook until soft. Add Basil. Add Oysters and cook for just one minute more.

2- In small sauce pan melt 1/4 lb. Butter, whisk in Flour then add Cream. Cook over low heat until it is smooth and thick.

3- Add Cream sauce to Mushrooms and Oysters. Stir and cook for one minute more. Adjust Salt and add a dash of crushed Red Pepper Flakes if you want this dish spicy.

4- Put in small chafing dish and serve with Garlic Toasts.

Ingredients for Oysters & Mushrooms

- 1 lb. Sliced Mushrooms
- 2 tbls. Butter
- 2 each Shallots
- 2 tbls. Minced Garlic
- 2 tbls. Minced Fresh Basil
- 1/4 lb. Butter
- 2 tbls. Flour
- 1 cup Cream
- 24 Shucked Oysters (ask for select East Coast Oysters)

Garlic Toast

Ingredients for Garlic Toast

- 2 loaves Thin Baguette
- 1/4 lb. Butter
- 2 tbls. Olive Oil
- 1 tbls. Minced Garlic
- 1 tbls. Minced Parsley
- 1 tbls. Paprika

MAKES 24 SERVINGS

1- Slice Baguette into rounds 1/2 inch thick and place on baking sheets.

2- In small sauce pan melt Butter, Olive Oil, Garlic and Parsley.

3- With pastry brush, brush Butter mixture on top of each Bread slice. Sprinkle a touch of Paprika on top of each slice.

4- Bake at 250 degrees until brown and crisp.

5- The Toasts should be served dry and crisp.

Toasts can be made ahead and stored in an airtight container.

Jalapeno Corn Muffins

MAKES 3 DOZEN MINI MUFFINS

1- In large mixing bowl, mix Corn Meal, Flour and Baking Powder.

2- In small bowl beat Eggs until smooth, add Milk and add to Flour mixture.

3- Add Oil, Jalapeno and Creamed Corn, mix well.

4- Spray muffin tins with Oil and fill half way.

5- Bake at 325 for 25-30 minutes.

6- When cool, cut in half and fill with Smoked Chicken Salad.

Ingredients for Jalapeno Corn Muffins	
1 cup	Yellow Corn Meal
1/2 cup	Flour
1 tbls.	Baking Powder
3	Eggs
3/4 cup	Milk
1/4 cup	Oil
3 tbls.	Minced Pickled Jalapeno
9 oz. can	Creamed Corn

Ingredients for Smoked Chicken Salad	
3 cups	Diced Smoked Chicken
1 cup	Diced Celery
1/2 cup	Mayonnaise
1 tbls.	Lime Juice
2 tbls.	Minced Fresh Basil
1/2 teas.	Salt
1/4 teas.	Pepper

Smoked Chicken Salad with Basil Mayonnaise

MAKES 5 CUPS

1- Be sure when you dice Chicken and Celery to keep in mind the size Muffins you are going to use. The smaller the Muffin, the smaller the dice. For mini Muffins you could make this Salad in the food processor.

2- In large mixing bowl add diced Smoked Chicken and diced Celery.

3- Mix Mayonnaise, Lime Juice, Basil, Salt and Pepper and add to Smoked Chicken.

4- Fill Corn Muffins.

Caramelized Onion & Roast Tomato Pastries

MAKES 2 DOZEN

1- Cut Roma Tomatoes into quarters, length-wise.
Place on baking sheet and sprinkle with Salt and Pepper.
Roast at 400 degrees until they begin to dry and brown,
about 30-35 minutes.

2- Peel Onion. Cut in half, then slice thin slices.
Put in very hot skillet. Push Onions around pan with wooden
spoon until they are browned evenly with a nice caramel
color. Add Salt and Pepper.

3- Cut 5x5 Puff Pastry squares into quarters. Place on baking
sheet and turn the corners up just a touch.

4- On each Pastry top with Caramelized Onion and a
Tomato quarter.

5- Bake at 350 degrees about 12 minutes until Pastry is
browned. Serve warm or room temperature.

Ingredients for Caramelized Onion & Roast Tomato Pastries

- 6 each   5x5 Puff Pastry Squares
- 6 each   Roma Tomato
- 1 lg.   Onion
-     Salt and Pepper

Pickled Shrimp

Ingredients for Pickled Shrimp

- 2 dz.   Large Gulf Shrimp
- 1/2 cup   Oil
- 1/2 teas.   Mustard Seed
- 1/2 cup   Red Wine Vinegar
- 2 tbls.   Dijon Mustard
- 2 tbls.   Minced Chives
- 2 tbls.   Minced Green Onion
- 1/2 teas.   Salt
- 1/2 teas.   Crushed Red Pepper

MAKES 2 DOZEN

1- Peel and devein Shrimp. Cook in boiling salted
water for about 2-3 minutes. Immediately rinse
with cold water and put ice on Shrimp.

2- Soak Mustard Seed in Red Wine Vinegar for 15
minutes.

3- In bowl mix Oil, Dijon Mustard, Chives, Green
Onions, Crushed Red Pepper and Salt. Whisk
together, then whisk in Vinegar and Mustard
Seed.

4- Toss Dressing with Shrimp and marinate for at
least two hours before serving.

5- Place in decorative serving bowl and garnish
with Lemon or Baby Gherkins or both.

This dish may be made the day before your party.

BOURBON PECAN CHOCOLATE TRUFFLES

1- In a sauce pan mix Cream, Butter, Corn Syrup and Bourbon together. Place over medium heat and bring to a full boil. Turn off heat immediately after this mixture comes to a boil

2- Make sure Chocolate is cut into small pieces. Add to mixture and gently stir it in and after it sits for about 5 minutes then whisk to make sure it is smooth.

3- Chop Pecans in food processor and stir into Truffle mixture.

4- Place in glass or metal bowl and refrigerate for about 40 minutes.

5- I use a small melon baller for size. Scoop out even portions and roll into ball.

6- Place back in refrigerator to set for at least 20 minutes.

7- Roll in Cocoa and keep chilled. Take out 30 minutes before serving.

Ingredients for Bourbon-Pecan Chocolate Truffles		
•	1 cup	Heavy Cream
•	4 tbls.	Unsalted Butter
•	1 tsp.	Light Corn Syrup
•	1 lb.	Semi-Sweet Chocolate, chopped
•	1 cup	Pecans
•	1 tbls.	Bourbon
•	1 cup	Dutch-process Cocoa Powder, sifted

I love having Parties but some times it is easier to feed a large group dinner than to do time consuming Hors d'oeuvre's. Here is a Menu that you can do for a large crowd that is fairly easy to do.

You can choose two appetizers from the Cocktail Menu and add this and have a Holiday Dinner Party instead of a Cocktail Party. On the next page you will find my recipe for "Cooking for a Crowd".

Cooking for a Crowd
Chicken and Italian Sausage Roast with Potatoes, Roasted Peppers and Corn

This recipe serves 20...just double for 40 etc. it is the perfect Dish for a crowd. It is not hard, not expensive and everyone loves it. The hardest part of this Dish is finding something large enough to serve it in.

You will also need large Roasting Pans. The old fashion Blue ones from the Hardware store are not expensive and work well for cooking and serving this dish. Much of this Dish can be made ahead and reheated before serving. The Corn should not be done until right before serving.

Preheat oven to 375 degrees

1- In large metal bowl add Chicken Thighs and Chicken Breasts. Add Dijon Mustard, Sea Salt, Cracked Black Pepper and Thyme. Toss until the Chicken is coated in the Mustard and Spices.

2- In two separate baking pans place Chicken Thighs in one and Cut Breasts in the other. Cut the Lemons and add to the Chicken.

3- Place Chicken Thighs in oven first for 15 minutes then place Breasts in oven and leave both in for another 30 minutes. (Thighs take 45 minutes and Breasts 30 minutes). Remove and let cool.

4- Place the Italian Sausage on a baking sheet and cook for 30 minutes. Let cool and cut each Link into three pieces. Save the drippings from the Sausage.

5- Place the Red Potatoes in a roasting pan and pour the Italian Sausage drippings over the Potatoes. Salt and Pepper the Potatoes. Add the Garlic Cloves and 5 Sprigs of Rosemary. Put in oven and roast for 45-55 minutes or until the Potatoes are easily pierced with a fork. Remove cooked Rosemary.

6- In Large Roasting Pan toss Chicken, Italian Sausage, Potatoes and Roasted Red Peppers together. Add the other five sprigs of Rosemary and Kalmata Olives. Heat in 350 degree oven for 30 minutes or until hot enough to serve. Make sure the Corn is done in time to be added to the dish before serving.

7- Clean Corn and snap in half. Bring a pot to a boil and cook until the Corn is tender. The Corn will be tossed in Olive Oil, Sea Salt and Black Pepper and tossed into the dish right before serving.

Ingredients for Chicken Sausage Roast with Potatoes, Corn and Peppers

- 10   Chicken Thighs (skin on and bone in)
- 8   Chicken Breasts (have your butcher cut the Breast into two to three pieces for you. Leave the bone in and skin on)
- 1 cup   Dijon Mustard
- 2 tbls.   Sea Salt
- 2 tbls.   Cracked Black Pepper
- 1 teas.   Garlic Powder
- 2 teas.   Thyme
- 12 links   Italian Sausage (Sweet or Hot which ever you prefer)
- 3 dozen   Small Red Potatoes
- 10 Ears   Yellow Sweet Corn
- 2 Cups   Roasted Red Peppers Cut into Strips (these are available in bottles and cans in the Italian Section of the Grocery)
- 16   Cloves of Garlic
- 10   Sprigs of Fresh Rosemary
- 1 cup   Pitted Kalmata Olives
- 2   Lemons

Salt and Cracked Black Pepper

Optional:
To Jazz this dish up for a more upscale party...you can add Slipper Lobster Tails or Jumbo Shrimp in the Shell. This adds to the price of the Dish considerably. You may want to do Shellfish for a smaller crowd.

Dinners for Two

Three Menus

Skewers with Potatoes, Brussels Sprouts
& Petite Blue Cheese stuffed Filet Mignon

or

Scalloped Potatoes
with Green Beans & Roasted Tomatoes
Shrimp wrapped in Pancetta

or

Salmon in Steamed Cabbage Leaves
with Caviar Toasts

Skewers with Potatoes, Brussels Sprouts & Petite Blue Cheese stuffed Filet Mignon

MAKES 2 SERVINGS

1- Take each 2 oz. Filet and cut the side to make a pocket, then fill with 1/2 oz. of Blue Cheese.

2- In boiling, salted water cook Brussels Sprouts about 4-5 minutes. You want them to be tender enough for a fork to go through easily.

3- Cook Potatoes until tender, but not too soft.

4- Using four metal skewers, put Brussels Sprout, Potato, Filet, Brussels Sprout, Potato, Filet on each skewer.

5- Place slices of Bacon on rimmed baking sheet, place in 400 degree oven for 12-14 minutes.

6- Let Bacon cool enough to handle and tightly wrap two slices around the food on each skewer.

7- Place skewers on a roasting rack that has been placed on a rimmed baking sheet. Put in 500 degree oven for 7 to 8 minutes if you prefer rare, 9 to 10 minutes for medium and 12 minutes for well done.

8- Leave on skewer to serve.

If you would like to garnish the plate you can slice Red Onion and Pears, toss in Vinegar, Oil and Salt and Sugar. It looks nice and is a great accompaniment to this dish. Walnuts are a nice addition to this one minute Salad.

Ingredients for Skewers of Potatoes, Brussels Sprouts and stuffed Filet Mignon

•	8	2 oz. Filets of Beef
•	4 oz.	Blue Cheese
•		Salt and Pepper
•	8	Brussels Sprouts
•	8	Baby Yukon Gold or Red Potatoes
•	8	Slices of Apple Cured Bacon

Optional for Garnish

•	1/2	Red Onion
•	1	Red Bartlett Pear
•	3 tbls.	Walnuts
•		Vinegar, Oil, Salt and Sugar

There is hardly a red wine that doesn't go with this dish...so I say this is the time to get into something new and different. A Spanish Rioja, Italian Sangiovese, a French Pomerol or an Australian Shiraz. If you want American try one of the many Meritages that are available, these are interesting blends made by many of our California wine makers.

SCALLOPED POTATOES WITH GREEN BEANS & ROASTED TOMATOES SHRIMP WRAPPED IN PANCETTA

MAKES 2 SERVINGS

Potatoes

1- Peel and slice Potatoes thin (1/8 inch slices).
2- Peel and slice Onion.
3- Sauté Onion in Butter until soft.
4- In small baking pan or skillet, layer Onion and Potatoes, Salt and Pepper between layers.
5- Top with Cream, cover with foil. Bake at 350 degrees for 40-50 minutes.

Green Beans

6- Quarter Roma Tomatoes length-wise. Place on baking sheet, sprinkle with Salt and Pepper. Roast in 400 degree oven until they begin to dry and brown.
7- Blanch Green Beans in boiling water for 4 minutes. Drain and rinse in cold water.

Shrimp

8- Cut each thin slice of Pancetta into two pieces, wrap around each Shrimp. Sprinkle with Pepper.

Completing the Dish

9- In hot skillet sauté the Shrimp, crisping the Pancetta. Squeeze fresh Lemon at the end.
10- In another sauté pan heat Olive Oil. Add Green Beans, Lemon Pepper, adding Tomatoes at the end.
11- On each dinner plate place a serving of the Scalloped Potatoes in the center (you may cut into a square, then into two triangles if you like).
12- Surround Potatoes with Green Beans and Tomatoes.
13- Arrange the four Shrimp around the Potatoes and on top of the Green Beans and Tomato. Serve immediately.

Ingredients for Scalloped Potato and Shrimp Dinner

Scalloped Potatoes

- 2   Idaho Potatoes
- 2 tbls.   Butter
- 1   Onion
- 3 tbls.   Cream

Salt and Pepper

Ingredients for Green Beans with Tomato

- 1/2 lb.   Cleaned Green Beans
- 4   Roma Tomatoes
- 1 teas.   Lemon Pepper
- 2 tbls.   Olive Oil

Ingredients for Shrimp wrapped in Pancetta

- 8   Large Gulf Shrimp
- 4   Paper thin slices of Pancetta
- 1/2 teas.   Cracked Black Pepper
- 1/2   Fresh Lemon

With this dish I recommend a Sancerre or Pinot Grigio if you prefer a light white wine. If you prefer a more intense finish in your white wines I recommend a Sauvignon Blanc.

SALMON IN STEAMED CABBAGE LEAVES WITH CAVIAR TOASTS

MAKES 2 SERVINGS

Preparing the Salmon in Steamed Cabbage Leaves

1- In pot of boiling, salted water blanch Cabbage Leaves for 2 minutes.

2- Drain and cool enough to handle.

3- Salt and Pepper Salmon Filets and wrap tightly in Cabbage Leaves.

4- Place in baking pan with 1/4 inch of water in the bottom of the pan. Cover with foil and place in 400 degree oven for 12-15 minutes. If you like a slight amount of pink left in the center of your Salmon Filet cook for 12 minutes.

Preparing the Butter Sauce

5- In sauté pan add Vinegar, White Wine, minced Shallot and Cream.

6- Reduce over medium heat. The reduction should be slightly moist, but no liquid should be remaining in the pan.

7- Cut cold Butter into six pieces. Gradually whisk in each piece of Butter, over low heat, to make a smooth Sauce. The Shallots remain in and give flavor and texture. *The Butter should not be separating. If it begins to separate, put Sauce back over the heat for a moment, then add a little more cold Butter, whisking in to make the Sauce smooth.*

Preparing the Caviar Toasts

8- Melt Butter and brush on sliced French Bread, toast in oven until brown and crisp.

9- Top with Crème Fraiche or a light Sour Cream then spoon Caviar on top.

Completing the Dish

10- With sharp knife, slice each Salmon Filet wrapped in Cabbage in half at a slight angle.

11- Place in center of each plate, placing one half of the Salmon on the other. Lace with Sauce. Then place Caviar Toasts around.

Champagne is wonderful with this dish.

Ingredients for Salmon in Steamed Cabbage Leaves with Caviar Toasts

Salmon in Cabbage

- 2 each   6 oz. Salmon Filet
- 1 head   Napa Cabbage
-    Salt and Pepper

Butter Sauce

- 2 tbls.   White Wine Vinegar
- 1 tbls.   White Wine
- 1 tbls.   Heavy Cream
- 1   Shallot
- 1/4 lb.   Butter (cold)

Caviar Toasts

- 8   Thin slices of French Bread
- 3 tbls.   Butter
- 4 tbls.   Crème Fraiche
- 1 oz.   Caviar

Since this dish is rich enough, you don't have to use the top of the line in Caviar. A Mandarin Caviar will do, even Black Lumpfish will do...but if you want to splurge - Osetra is my choice.

Christmas Dinner Buffet

Menu

Meats
Crown Rack of Lamb
Prime Rib Roast
Quail and Mushroom Pie

Side Dishes
Savory Bread Pudding
Mashed Potatoes with White Truffle Butter
Creamed Spinach with Jalapeno
Brussels Sprouts with Smoked Bacon and Grain Mustard
Marinated Green Beans with Peppadew in
Preserved Lemon Vinaigrette

Condiments
Cranberry-Mango Chutney
Tomato-Mint Marmalade
Horseradish Sauce

Desserts
Chocolate-Orange Mousse
Cranberry-Gingerbread Trifle with Praline Sauce
Assorted Dessert Cheeses and French Walnuts

CROWN RACK OF LAMB

MAKES 6 SERVINGS
Use heavy roasting pan.
Preheat oven to 425 Degrees.

1- In small sauce pan melt Butter adding Brandy, Garlic, Mustard, Thyme, Salt and Pepper to create the Marinade.
2- Set Crown Roast of Lamb in roasting pan and season the Lamb with the Marinade.
3-To roast Lamb place in 425 degree oven.

To cook your Roast to desired temperature-
Rare   10-minutes per pound (125 degrees/51 c)
Medium   12-minutes per pound (140 degrees/60 c)
Well Done   14-minutes per pound (160 degrees/70 c)

4- Remove Lamb from pan and place on serving platter. Leave on top of stove so it stays warm.
5- Pour one cup of Water into roasting pan to deglaze Lamb drippings. Try to remove as much fat as possible by skimming with a spoon.
6- In sauté pan with 1 tbls. Butter, sauté minced Shallots. Add Lamb drippings and continue to cook over medium heat.
7- Add Port, Green Peppercorn, continue to cook.
8- In small bowl or cup add 1 tbls. Corn Starch to 3 tbls. Water and make a smooth paste. Add it to the Sauce.
9- Continue to simmer until your Sauce begins to thicken.

Serve in gravy dish to accompany Lamb.

Ingredients for Crown Roast of Lamb		
•	4 lb.	Crown Roast of Lamb
•	4 cloves	Minced Garlic
•	1/4 lb.	Butter
•	1 tbls.	Brandy
•	2 tbls.	Dijon Mustard
•	1 teas.	Thyme
•	1 tbls.	Sea Salt
•		Pepper to taste
Ingredients for Green Peppercorn Sauce		
•	2	Shallots
•	1/4 cup	Port
•	2 tbls.	Green Peppercorns
•	2 cups	Degreased Lamb Drippings
•	1 tbls.	Corn Starch
•	3 tbls.	Water
•	1 tbls.	Butter

PRIME RIB ROAST

Ingredients for Prime Rib of Beef		
•	8 lb.	Boneless Ribeye of Beef
•	8 cloves	Garlic
•	1/4 lb.	Butter
•	3 tbls.	Worcestershire Sauce
•	2 tbls.	Brandy
•	1 teas.	Garlic Powder
•	1 teas.	Onion Powder
•	1 teas.	Thyme
•	1 teas.	Basil
•	3 or 4 tbls.	Coarse Ground Sea Salt

MAKES 10-12 SERVINGS
Use heavy Roasting Pan.

1- Using a boning knife make 16 punctures into the Beef. Cut the cloves of Garlic in half length-wise and put into puncture holes in Beef.

2- In small saucepan melt Butter adding Worcestershire Sauce, Brandy, Garlic Powder, Onion Powder, Thyme and Basil.

3- Let Butter mixture cool down. Then pour over the Beef slowly so the mixture can find its way into the puncture holes.
4- Rub Salt on.

To Roast Beef-
Preheat oven to 450 Degrees
Put Beef Ribeye in for 15 minutes at 450 degrees
After 15 minutes turn oven down to 350 Degrees

To cook your Roast to desired temperature-
Rare   12-14 minutes per pound (125 degrees/ 51 c)
Medium   15-17 minutes per pound (140 degrees/ 60 c)
Well Done   17-20 minutes per pound (160 degrees/ 70 c)

Check temperature with a meat thermometer and remember the Meat will continue to cook for a few minutes after you remove it from the oven. Let rest 15 minutes before carving.

Quail and Mushroom Pie

MAKES 6 Servings

1- Prepare your copper pan or pie pan with Pie Pastry.
2- Season Quail with Salt, Pepper and Garlic Powder.
3- Dice the Carrots and Potatoes into a small dice approximately half inch. Cook the diced Carrots and Potatoes until done but not too soft.
4- Place cast iron skillet over medium-high heat. Let skillet get hot, then add diced Bacon and cook until done. Remove Bacon and immediately add Mushrooms and sauté. Remove Mushrooms and place in a bowl with the Bacon. Toss the cooked Carrots and Potatoes with the Bacon and Mushrooms.
5- Pour out Bacon Grease, but leave just enough in the skillet for the Quail not to stick to the pan.
6- Add the Quail and brown well, lower heat and continue to cook the Quail until they are done. Remove from skillet and let cool enough to remove all the Meat from the bones. Dice in even pieces, approx. 1/2 inch dice.
7- While skillet is still hot add diced Shallots and Garlic then sauté for 1 minute. Add Water to deglaze the pan and then add the Port. Remove Thyme from stem and add. Simmer for 15 minutes.
8- Make a paste with 2 tbls. Cornstarch and 1/4 cup of Water. Add to skillet and stir until dissolved and sauce begins to thicken.
9- Add diced Quail to Sauce and stir in Mushrooms, Bacon, Carrots and Potatoes. Let cool before filling pie pasty.
10- Pour into 9 inch pie pastry or 1 qt. copper baking dish. Top with Pastry.
11- Bake at 350 degrees until crust is golden brown approx. 45 minutes.

Ingredients for Quail and Mushroom Pie

•		Pie Pastry for top and bottom.
•	8	Semi Boneless Quail

Salt, Pepper, Garlic Powder

•	2	Slices of Smoked Bacon
•	2	Shallots
•	1/2 cup	Diced Carrots
•	1 cup	Diced Red Potatoes
•	1/2 cup	Water
•	1 cup	Ruby Port
•	4	Cloves Garlic
•	3	Sprigs of Thyme
•	2 tbls.	Cornstarch
•	2 tbls.	Water
•	1 lb.	Mushrooms

Ingredients for Savory Bread Pudding

•	1 lb.	Ground Italian Sausage with Fennel
•	1/2 cup	Diced Onion
•	1/2 cup	Diced Celery
•	1/4 cup	Diced Bell Pepper
•	2 tbls.	Garlic
•	6 cups	Cubed Bread
•	4	Eggs
•	1 cup	Cream
•	1/2 teas.	Sage

Salt and Pepper if needed usually the Sausage has enough seasoning

Savory Bread Pudding

MAKES 10-12 SERVINGS
You will need a 9x13 baking dish or a 2 qt. Soufflé dish.

1- In large sauté pan brown ground Sausage, drain off excess fat.

2- Add Onion, Celery, Bell Pepper and Garlic and sauté with Sausage until Vegetables are soft.

3- In large bowl add Sausage mixture to cubed Bread and toss.

4- Beat Eggs and Cream together and add Sage. Add to Sausage and Bread mixture.

5- Pour into Oiled baking dish and bake at 350 degrees for 40-45 minutes.

Mashed Potatoes with White Truffle Butter

MAKES 12 SERVINGS
Have a colander in the sink and have an electric hand mixer close by. Even if you have to use an extension cord it is best to whip the Potatoes over a burner on the stove.
You can make these up to two hours ahead of serving time.

1- Wash and peel the Yukon Gold Potatoes.

2- Cut Potatoes in equal size pieces. 2x1 inch cubes work well.

3- Place Potatoes in large pot and cover with cold water and bring to a boil. Turn to medium heat and cook until tender, about 20 minutes.

4- While Potatoes are cooking take Butter and soften to room temperature. You may microwave at 20 second intervals to speed the process.

5- In Mixing Bowl, whip Butter and slowly add Truffle Oil.

6- When the Potatoes are done, drain them in a colander and cover with a dish towel to help hold in the heat. Let stand for at least 5 minutes. The Potatoes must be dry.

7- Pour the Potatoes back into the pot and whip with the electric mixer. Add the Sour Cream and Truffle Butter and whip until you have fluffy, smooth potatoes. Begin to season with Salt and White Pepper. Taste and adjust the seasoning.

Serve immediately or put in glass serving bowl that can be microwaved. Cover with plastic wrap and set aside.
Microwave (with plastic wrap on) for 4-5 minutes.
Remove plastic wrap and serve.

Ingredients for Mashed Potatoes with White Truffle Butter

- 4 lbs.   Yukon Gold Potatoes
- 2 lb.   Butter (salted)
- 3 1/2 oz.   White Truffle Oil
- 1 cup   Sour Cream

Salt and White Pepper to taste

I recommend two teaspoons of Salt and a half teaspoon of White Pepper to start and adjust from there.

Tomato Mint Marmalade

1- When dicing Tomatoes first cut the Tomatoes in quarters. Remove the seeds. Then dice in 1/4 inch pieces.
2- Julienne the fresh Mint.
3- In sauce pan add Orange Marmalade, Cider Vinegar and Brown Sugar. Cook until it is a syrup.
4- Add the Tomatoes and cook until the excess water from the Tomatoes reduce. This takes about 20 minutes.
5- Add the fresh Mint and stir.
6- This should be served warm or room temperature.
This keeps well in the refrigerator or freezer.

Ingredients for Tomato Mint Marmalade

- 1/2 cup   Orange Marmalade
- 2 cups   Finely Diced Fresh Tomato
- 1/2 cup   Fresh Mint
- 2 tbls.   Cider Vinegar
- 1 tbls.   Brown Sugar

BRUSSELS SPROUTS WITH SMOKED BACON GRAIN-MUSTARD SAUCE

MAKES 12 SERVINGS

1- Cut off white stem part of each Brussels Sprout.

2- In pot of salted boiling water put Sprouts in for 10 minutes or until tender.

3- Dice Bacon and cook in cast iron skillet until almost crisp. Drain most of the oil out of the pan.

4- Drain Brussels Sprouts well, then add to skillet and add Mustard. Toss well with Bacon and Mustard. Salt and Pepper to taste.

5- Add Cream and reduce for 5 minutes until Cream thickens and coats the Brussels Sprouts

This can be made ahead and reheated in a serving dish.

Ingredients for Brussels Sprouts with Smoked Bacon-Grain Mustard Sauce

- 2 lbs.   Brussels Sprouts
- 1/4 lb.   Bacon
- 4 tbls.   Whole Grain Mustard
- 1/4 cup   Cream

Salt and Pepper

MARINATED GREEN BEANS WITH PEPPADEW IN PRESERVED LEMON VINAIGRETTE

SERVES 12

1- Blanch and drain fresh Green Beans.

2- Drain Peppadew Peppers and cut into quarters.

3- Marinate Green Beans and Peppadews in Preserved Lemon Vinaigrette for two to three hours before serving.

4- When ready to serve, arrange mixed Baby Greens on serving platter and top with marinated Green Beans and Peppadew.

Ingredients for Marinated Green Beans with Peppadew in Preserved Lemon Vinaigrette

- 4 cups   Blanched Green Beans
- 1 cup   Peppadew cut into quarters
- 1 cup   Preserved Lemon Vinaigrette (page 168)
- 1 lb.   Mixed Baby Greens

CHOCOLATE-ORANGE MOUSSE

To Make the Mousse

1- In double boiler melt Chocolate, Coffee and Butter. Add Grated Orange Peel and Grand Marnier.

2- Put Egg Yolks and Sugar into small bowl and mix on medium speed until Yolks are pale yellow or ribbon stage.

3- Add the Yolk mixture to Chocolate mixture and continue to cook. Stir frequently over medium heat in double boiler, about 12-15 minutes. Remove from heat and transfer to another bowl. Let cool down for 10 minutes.

4- Beat the Egg Whites until they are stiff but not dry. Gently fold in the Egg Whites (a rubber spatula is the essential tool when doing this). Fold gently, you want the air to stay in the whipped Egg Whites to make the Mousse light.

5- Pour Chocolate Mousse into pretty clear glass Trifle bowl.

6- Lightly cover with plastic wrap and refrigerate for at least four hours before serving.

Ingredients for Chocolate-Orange Mousse	
8 oz.	Dark Sweet Chocolate
1 tbls.	Strong Coffee
2 tbls.	Grand Marnier
1/4 lb.	Butter
3	Eggs (separated)
3/4 cup	Sugar
2 tbls.	Grated Orange Peel

CRANBERRY-GINGERBREAD TRIFLE

MAKES 1 QUARTS

1- To make a Trifle you simply layer Cake, Custard and Whipped Cream. You can make in Trifle bowl or in individual servings.

2- Garnish with Sugared Cranberries and Cinnamon Sugar.

Ingredients for Cranberry-Gingerbread Trifle	
3 cups	Crème Brulee Custard (recipe on page 205)
3 cups	Cranberry Gingerbread Cake (recipe on page 191)
3 cups	Cinnamon Whipped Cream (recipe on page 191)

New Years Eve

Menu

Antipasta Tray
Pepper Salami, Roasted Peppers, Assorted Cheeses, Olives

Cioppino
with Spanish Chorizo, Clams and Red Snapper

Crepes Suzette

CIOPPINO

This dish is influenced by my years in San Francisco but has my twist on a San Francisco favorite.
When you buy your fish for this dish ask if the fish head and bones from your Red Fish are available. This will make your Stock much better for your Cioppino. This dish is still very good if you don't add the Fish Stock and just add Water because of the other flavors from the Chorizo and Fennel.
The Spanish Style Chorizo is a key ingredient as well. It can be found in specialty grocery stores such as Whole Food or at www.BattistoniBrand.com

1- Place 6 qt. soup pot on medium heat.

2- Add diced Chorizo and cook until it sizzles and pops, then add Onion, Bell Pepper and sauté for three minutes.

3- Add 3 qts. of Fish Stock or Water and bring to a boil.

4- Lower heat to a simmer and add Tomato Paste and Dark Roux and stir until dissolved.

5- Add Diced Tomatoes, Garlic, Fennel Seeds, Dry Basil, Saffron Threads and crushed Red Pepper Flakes.

6- Simmer for one hour.

7- Add Clams one half hour before serving. Add the Fish just ten minutes before serving and the Crab Claws five minutes before serving. Bring to a boil and serve right away.

Ingredients for Cioppino	
8 oz.	Chorizo (Spanish Style Sausage) Diced
1	Medium White Onion Fine Dice
1	Red Bell Pepper Diced
3 qts.	Fish Stock or Water
1/2 cup	Tomato Paste
1/2 cup	Dark Roux (recipe page 236)
12 oz.	Canned Diced Tomatoes
4 tbls.	Minced Garlic
2 teas.	Fennel Seeds
1 tbls.	Dry Basil
1/2 teas.	Saffron Threads
2 teas.	Crushed Red Pepper
2 lbs.	Small Clams in the Shell (scrub well)
3 lbs.	Red Fish 2 inch cubes
2 lbs.	Shelled Blue Crab Claws

ANTIPASTA TRAY

SERVES 12

1- Cut heads of Radicchio into quarters.

2- Drain the Marinated Cheese- but save the Oil it is packed in.

3- Toss the Radicchio in the seasoned Oil the Cheese was packed in.

4- Get an iron skillet very hot and add the Radicchio to roast but do not over cook.

5- On large serving platter, place the Radicchio in the center of the platter. Top with Marinated Cheese.

6- Slice Pepper Salami in thin rounds. Arrange around the Radicchio.

7- Slice Roasted Peppers into 1/4 inch slices and arrange next to the Salami.

8- Slice the Aged Parmesan Cheese into nice shaved pieces and arrange on platter.

9- Garnish with Smoked Mozzarella and Assorted Olives.

Ingredients for Antipasta Tray	
3 heads	Radicchio
1 cup	Marinated Blue Cheese or Feta Cubes
1 lb.	Pepper Salami
1 cup	Roasted Peppers
1 lb.	Aged Parmesan Cheese
1 lb.	Smoked Mozzarella
1 cup	Assorted Olives

CREPES SUZETTE

MAKES 14-16

1- In a large mixing bowl, whisk together the Flour and the Eggs. Gradually add in the Milk and Water, stirring to combine. Add the Salt and Butter, beat until smooth.

2- Heat a lightly oiled 6 or 7 inch non stick Egg pan over medium-high heat. I usually use two at once to make this process quick. Pour or scoop the batter onto the griddle, using approximately 1/4 cup for each Crepe. Tilt the pan with a circular motion so that the Batter coats the surface evenly.

3- Cook the Crepe for about 2 minutes, until the bottom is light brown. Loosen with a spatula, turn and cook the other side.

To Make the Sauce

1- Grate the Orange Peel of three Oranges. Do not get the white pith.

2- Add 1 cup of Sugar to the Grated Rind. Let sit for one hour.

3- In a sauté pan add the Butter and slowly melt. Do not brown the Butter.

4- Add the Sugar and Orange Peel and, stirring constantly with a wooden spoon, cook until the Sugar completely dissolves.

5- Fold the Crepes into quarters and gently set into Orange Sauce.

6- Add the Grand Marnier, carefully, it will flame up. Let it flame and reduce down for about a minute.

Serve right away.

Ingredients for Crepes

- 2 cups   Flour
- 4   Eggs
- 1 cup   Milk
- 1 cup   Water
- 1/2 teas.   Salt
- 4 tbls.   Melted Unsalted Butter

I often use Salted Butter and do not add Salt.

Sauce for Crepes

- 3   Oranges
- 1 cup   Sugar
- 1/2 lb.   Butter
- 1/2 cup   Grand Marnier Liqueur

Lagniappe...a little something extra.

Here towards the end of the book I have decided to add a few extras that hopefully will help you in your cooking and ease of entertaining. I am including some basic Stock and Sauce recipes that might help you in your cooking. I have added a few recipes that were not in a specific Menu that I thought you would like to have. I also am adding a temperature and conversion chart. Most importantly, I have included my list of ingredients that I try to keep on hand at all times. I entertain quite a bit and I do not like going to the grocery store. If you keep a well stocked (not over stocked) pantry your trips to the store can be a bit briefer and you may find yourself being a bit more spontaneous about having guests for a simple dinner.

SMOKED TOMATOES AND SMOKED SEA SALT

1- Soak Hickory Chips for 1 hour.

2- Get grill hot, it is easier to use a gas grill. If you have a charcoal grill you want to wait until your coals are completely grey and are beginning to get cooler, not at their maximum heat.

3- Quarter Roma Tomatoes and toss with Olive Oil, Sea Salt and Cracked Black Pepper. Place in a disposable aluminum baking pan.

4- Pour the pound of Coarse Sea Salt in another disposable aluminum baking pan.

5- Add Hickory chips to coals.

6- Place both pans on grill and close the lid.

7- Let smoke for at least one hour.

I let the Smoked Tomatoes cool and I freeze them for later use. When they are freshly done, I use them for Salads.

When the Smoked Sea Salt cools put in a plastic container with a lid to keep moisture out, or a small Ziploc bag.

Ingredients for Smoked Tomatoes

- 5 lbs.   Roma Tomatoes
- 2 tbls.   Sea Salt
- 1 tbls.   Cracked Black Pepper
- 1/2 cup   Olive Oil

Ingredients for Smoked Sea Salt

- 1 lb.   Coarse Sea Salt
- 1 lb.   Hickory Chips

BROWN SAUCE
DEMI GLACE

1- Preheat the oven to 450 degrees F. Place the Bones in a roasting pan and roast for 1 hour. Remove the Bones from the oven and brush with the Tomato Paste.

2- In a mixing bowl, combine the Onions, Carrots, and Celery together. Lay the Vegetables over the Bones and return to the oven. Roast for 30 minutes. Remove from the oven and drain off any fat.

3- Place the roasting pan on the stove and deglaze the pan with the Red Wine, using a wooden spoon, scraping the bottom of the pan for browned particles. Put everything into a large stockpot. Season with Salt, Pepper and fresh Thyme

4- Add the Water. Bring the liquid up to a boil and reduce to a simmer. Simmer the Stock for 4 hours, skimming regularly. Remove from the heat and strain through a China cap or tightly meshed strainer.

Yield: about 2 gallons. I reduce this by half again to make 1 gallon. I freeze in pint containers and use for various sauces.

Ingredients for Brown Sauce Demi Glace

- 8 lbs.   Veal Marrow Bones sawed into 2-inch pieces
- 6 lbs.   Beef Marrow Bones sawed into 2-inch pieces
- 16 oz.   Tomato Paste
- 4 cups   Chopped Onions
- 2 cups   Chopped Carrots
- 2 cups   Chopped Celery
- 4 cups   Red Wine
- 5 sprigs   Fresh Thyme
- 16 quarts   Water

Salt and Pepper

DARK ROUX

How to make a Dark Roux-the time is worth the effort...the better the Roux...the better your dish.
- 1/2 cup Oil
- 1 cup Flour

In a cast iron skillet, heat Oil over medium heat until just smoking. Whisk in Flour, a little at a time and cook, whisking constantly, until Roux becomes smooth and thick. Continue to cook, constantly stirring with a spoon and reaching all over bottom of pan, until Roux darkens to a rich brown nutty color, about 25 minutes. Remove from the heat and put into a metal bowl and it will continue to cook but not burn..it will become a chocolate brown...which I find to be the perfect Roux.

236

BÉCHAMEL
(WHITE SAUCE)

1- In a medium heavy pan, melt Butter over low heat. When Butter starts to foam, add the Flour all at once, mixing well with a whisk. Cook over low heat 3 to 4 minutes, stirring constantly to incorporate and cook Flour. Remove pan from heat and let stand, up to 15 minutes.

2- In a medium saucepan, scald Milk (heating it until just below boiling point).

3- Return pan with Roux to medium-low heat. Add all of the scalded Milk at once (to avoid the formation of lumps). Simmer, stirring gently with a wire whisk or wooden spoon.

4- Add studded Onion and Bay Leaf. Cook, stirring, over low heat, 15 to 20 minutes, until smooth and thickened. Strain sauce through fine-mesh strainer. Add Salt, White Pepper and Nutmeg to taste. Makes about 2 cups.

Ingredients for Béchamel Sauce

- 1/4 cup   Unsalted Butter
- 1/4 cup   Flour
- 2 cups   Milk
- 1   Onion studded with 2 Cloves
- 1   Small Bay Leaf

Salt and White Pepper to taste
Nutmeg, to taste- depending on what I am using the Sauce for.

BUERRE BLANC AND
BUERRE ROUGE

Ingredients for Butter Sauce

Buerre Blanc-White Wine Sauce

Buerre Rouge-Red Wine Sauce

- 1/4 cup   White Wine Vinegar
- 1/4 cup   White Wine
- 1 medium   Shallot
- 3 tbls.   Cream
- 1/2 lb.   Butter

For Red Wine Sauce-

Use Red Wine Vinegar and Red Wine instead of White.

1- In 10 or 12 inch sauté pan add Vinegar, Wine, Shallots and Cream. Reduce until thick. This takes about 10-14 minutes. I add the Cream as a stabilizer, it helps insure your Sauce won't break as easy.

2- When reduced take away from flame. Cut Butter into tablespoon sized pieces.

3- Place the pan over a low heat. Begin whisking in the Butter a little at a time. The Butter should melt into a Cream so it forms an emulsion instead of melting into an Oil.

4- The finished Sauce can be heated rapidly to help set the Sauce.

5- Store in a Bain Marie (double boiler) with tepid water. Keep away from excessive heat. This Sauce should hold for up to 90 minutes before using it.

Being Spontaneous takes a lot of planning... Spontaneous cooking takes having the right ingredients at your fingertips to allow you artistic freedom. This is a list of items to keep on hand in your kitchen to help you be more spontaneous in your cooking. With the right items on hand you will be able to take whatever is in Season and create a Menu when you get home from your local farmers market. Even without fresh Produce you can create a few meals from this list with a quick run into the market for Meat or Fish and a few Salad Greens.

These items have a long shelf life and will not go bad. Most of these dairy items last for two weeks or more.

DAIRY
BUTTER
EGGS
AGED CHEESE– PARMEASEAN, ROMANO
SHARP CHEDDAR OR GOAT CHEESE
ANY OTHER CHEESE YOU MAY LIKE
CREAM CHEESE

HEAVY CREAM (always have a half pint on hand—it will keep for 7-10 days)

DRY GOODS
SUNDRIED TOMATOES
CANNED DICED TOMATOES
OLIVES
ROASTED PEPPERS
LIQUID SMOKE
SEA SALT
CRACKED BLACK PEPPER

DRY PASTA–
PENNE OR SMALL SHELL
LINGUINE OR SPAGHETTI
FLAVORED PASTAS ARE A GOOD ITEM TO PICK UP FROM GOURMET SHOPS–
(BLACK PEPER, SUNDRIED TOMATO ARE JUST A FEW OF THE FLAVORS ON THE MARKET)

RICE
LONG GRAIN OR BASMATI
RISOTTO

OLIVE OIL
CANOLA OR VEGETABLE OIL
VINEGAR-RED WINE OR CIDER AND BASALMIC

MISC. ITEMS
SMOKED BACON
CHICKEN STOCK
VEAL OR BEEF STOCK
CHOPPED ROASTED GARLIC

IN YOUR FREEZER
VANILLA ICE CREAM
TWO LOAVES OF GOOD BREAD (HERB BREAD, ROSEMARY BREAD, OLIVE BREAD AND A FRENCH BREAD)
FROZEN GREEN PEAS (pasta or risotto carbonara)
FROZEN CHOPPED SPINACH (to make a Florentine pasta or risotto or to make creamed spinach for a quick omelet with farm fresh eggs)

TEMPERATURE CHARTS AND CONVERSION CHARTS

Sugar Temperatures

	Approx.
Soft ball	234-240/113c
Firm ball	244-250/118c
Hard ball	250-265/122c
Light crack	270-290/125c
Hard crack	300-310/146c

For Perfect Eggs you need a perfect pan, non stick that you only use to cook your Eggs in.

For better color on your Meats and Fish, always get your pan very hot before you add your Meat or Fish. This will also add more flavor to your Sauces when you deglaze the pan (or add liquid to the pan).

Liquid Standards

			Approx.
3 teas.	= 1 tbls.	= 1/2 oz.	= 15 ml.
6 teas.	= 2 tbls.	= 1 oz.	= 30 ml.
16 tbls.	= 1 cup	= 8 oz.	= 250 ml.
2 cups	= 1 pint	= 16 oz.	= 500 ml.
2 pints	= 1 qt.	= 32 oz.	= 1 ltr.
2 qt.	= 1/2 gal.	= 64 oz.	= 2 ltr.
8 pints	= 4 qt.	= 1 gal.	= 4 ltr.

Dry Weights

			Approx.
1 cup Flour	= 4 oz.	= 1/4 lb.	= 125 gr.
1 cup Sugar	= 6.5 oz.	= 4/10 lb.	= 200 gr.
1 cup Butter	= 8 oz.	= 1/2 lb.	= 250 gr.

To Roast Meats

Preheat oven to 450 degrees, put meat into oven for 15 minutes then turn oven down to 350 degrees

To cook to your desired temperature

Rare	12-14 minutes per lb.	125 degrees/51c
Medium	15-17 minutes per lb.	140 degrees/60c
Well	17-19 minutes per lb.	160 degrees/70c

Check temperature with a meat thermometer, the Meat will continue to cook for a few minutes after you remove it from the oven. Let Meat rest for 15 minutes before carving.

Index

Index

241

Index

Index

THE HISTORY OF TWIN OAKS

The original land purchase was acquired from Jeremiah Routh and Robert Cochran and was part of their original Spanish land grants. The original cottage on the property (which is now the back kitchen and den area) was built around 1806 for Lewis Evans, the first Territorial Sheriff. In 1814 Evans sold the property to Jonathan Thompson, and in 1820 it was bought by Dr. Josiah Morris who fell victim to yellow fever and died just three years later. Dr. Morris' widow remarried and in 1832 sold the house to a young couple from Philadelphia, Pennsylvania, Pierce and Cornelia Connelly. The Connellys came to Natchez when Pierce became Rector of Trinity Episcopal Church. It is likely that the Connellys who added the original Greek Revival portion of the current structure since they sold their home for eight and half times more than they paid for it. In 1835 Cornelia Connelly named her home White Cottage which marked the completion of their addition. Shortly after this Pierce Connelly decided to leave the Episcopal Church and convert to Roman Catholicism. Although they were married and had four living children, the Connellys left Natchez and eventually went to Rome, where Pierce was ordained a Priest and Cornelia became a Nun. Leaving her children in orphanages, she was sent to England by the Pope, where Cornelia founded the Society of the Holy Child Jesus, an order of Nuns dedicated to teaching young girls. There are many books written about their unconventional lives. Dr. Frederick A. W. Davis owned the home at the time of the disastrous Tornado of 1840 which demolished the upper story. Charles L. Dubuisson purchased the damaged house in 1841 and by 1852 had completed the reconstructed Greek Revival house you see today.

Charles L. Dubuisson had served as President of Jefferson College then later became a Judge and Representative in the Mississippi State Legislature. After his three year old daughter drowned in a cistern on the property and his wife died of yellow fever shortly after that, he went into a deep depression and spent most of his time at his plantation in Yazoo County. Twin Oaks passed into the hands of Mrs. W.H. Dunbar and she was residing at White Cottage when the Federal gunboat shelled Natchez in 1862. Shortly after the Civil War a wealthy merchant, Mr. H.M. Gastrell, owned and loved this house for many years. He left it to his niece Maude K. Barton and she and her family continued to live here long after his death. The back part of the house, which was built in the early 1800's, had a fire during the 1870's and that is when the "Victorian" touches were added including the French doors going out to the gallery.

After the Whittingtons bought the house in 1940 and lovingly restored it, they extended and enclosed the back galleries, using windows from the old Natchez Cotton Mill which was being demolished at the time. This addition joined the two houses and provided more comfortable living spaces. The Whittingtons enjoyed and shared this house with Natchez and visitors from all over for over sixty years.

We purchased it in 2002 and have begun the restoration process all over again. As each family that called this house a home, we too have put our touches to make it our own. Many wonderful meals and memories are being made as we enjoy our home with our family and friends.

TWIN OAKS *was originally named White Cottage but when Dr. Whittington purchased the aging property in 1940 and began to renovate the house to its original beauty he said "It's not white and it is too grand to be called a Cottage" so he renamed it for the magnificent Oaks framing the house, "Twin Oaks".*

Through the years and generations each family that has lived in this house has added their personal touches to call it their own but most importantly to call it their home.

Special Thanks:

Janet Tyler, who not only helps me with everything I do and is so loving to all who walk through the doors of Twin Oaks, but most importantly she loves and spoils my boys and that is priceless.

Robert Jones, who makes the grounds of Twin Oaks so inviting and lovely.

Walter Davis, who is a book in himself and the truest of friends.

Jenna Aldridge, for genuine friendship and always my right hand...(and the Camera).

Kevin Brodeur and Kevin Miers at South Union Interiors for all you do.

For my coffee/poker group- Jerry, Mae-Mae, Jimmy Ray, Walter, Al, Larry B., Ty, Daryl, Hiram, George, Richie, Ron, Ed, Doc, Bob, Gloria, Mac, Cappy and Roy for being so appreciative of whatever I serve you and being a great bunch of friends.

Doris Ann Benoist, for entertaining me with so many "Dips", my only friend who has gotten through life without ever making an entrée.

Always my Sisters and Brothers -Ree, Andree, Phillip, Peter, Mary, Michelle, Finley and Ellen for being family and showing me how special that is.

Mark and Dixie Smitherman, for helping with pre-press and teaching me so much.

Fran Gealer, for the use of the loveliest photo of the hot pepper jelly torta on page 111.

Paige Porter Fischer, for writing such a lovely forward that my coffee group said they will use it as my eulogy.

"My Family" -Doug, Luc, Martin and Catherine, for having whatever I was cooking for dinner for the past months...I am now taking requests again until the Biscuit Book.

Kenneth Ross, a great friend and thanks for helping me with those final touches on the book.

My Chicago buddies....thank you....

All my friends who I dearly love-you know who you are.

First Edition 2007   ISBN 978-0-9800591-0-6

Photography by Fran Gealer located on page 111 (Hot Pepper Jelly Torta) and page 113 (Wedding Flowers and Gospel Singers) www.frangealer.com
All other photos were taken by Regina Charboneau www.reginaskitchen.com

reginacharboneau@yahoo.com
www. reginaskitchen.com

Regina's Table Press LLC
Natchez, MS. 391